10 Perspectives on Equity in Education

In this third volume of the Routledge *Great Educators Series*, ten of education's inspiring thought-leaders come together to bring you their perspectives on how to improve equitable outcomes in your school or classroom, so that all students have what they need to succeed. You will learn how to overcome barriers to equity of access; embrace a student's cultural capital; attract and retain a diverse talent pool; incorporate inter-sectional identities in an inclusive classroom; implement more equit-able assessment practices; build resilience and equity through chess; advance equity in early childhood programs; abolish a culture of com-petition and work toward a culture of cooperation; and increase stake-holder commitment to racial equity. Appropriate for K–12 educators at all levels, the book provides strategies, insights, and inspiration to help you lead for equity and make real changes in your classroom, building, and community.

Jimmy Casas (@casas_jimmy) served 22 years as a school leader, including 14 years as principal at Bettendorf High School in Bettendorf, Iowa. Under his leadership, Bettendorf was named one of the "Best High Schools" in the country three times by *Newsweek* and *US News & World Report*. Jimmy is the owner and CEO of J Casas & Associates, an educational leadership com-pany aimed at organizing and providing world-class professional coaching and learning services for educators across the country.

Onica L. Mayers (@O_L_Mayers) currently serves as a director for pro-fessional staffing and employee relations for human resources in the third largest school district in Texas. In her 22-year educational journey, she has served as a classroom teacher, instructional coach, assistant principal and elementary school principal for six years. She was recognized as the 2018 Elementary Principal of the Year and is currently a doctoral candidate at the University of Houston.

Jeffrey Zoul (@Jeff_Zoul) is a lifelong teacher, learner, and leader. During Jeff's distinguished career in education he has served in a variety of roles, most recently as assistant superintendent for teaching and learning with Deerfield Public Schools District 109 in Deerfield, Illinois. Jeff has been recognized as a local teacher of the year and as an outstanding principal in the State of Georgia. He also served as principal at a national School of Excellence in Illinois.

Routledge Great Educators Series

10 Perspectives on Innovation in Education
Edited by Jimmy Casas, Todd Whitaker, and Jeffrey Zoul

10 Perspectives on Learning in Education
Edited by Jimmy Casas, Todd Whitaker, and Jeffrey Zoul

10 Perspectives on Equity in Education
Edited by Jimmy Casas, Onica L. Mayers, and Jeffrey Zoul

For more information about this series, please visit:
www.routledge.com/Routledge-Great-Educators-Series/
book-series/RGE

10 Perspectives on Equity in Education

Edited by Jimmy Casas, Onica L. Mayers, and Jeffrey Zoul

Routledge
Taylor & Francis Group

NEW YORK AND LONDON

First published 2021
by Routledge
605 Third Avenue, New York, NY 10158

and by Routledge
2 Park Square, Milton Park, Abingdon, Oxon OX14 4RN

Routledge is an imprint of the Taylor & Francis Group, an informa business

Library of Congress Cataloging-in-Publication Data
Names: Casas, Jimmy, editor. | Mayers, Onica L., editor. | Zoul, Jeffrey, editor.
Title: 10 perspectives on equity in education/edited by Jimmy Casas,
Onica L. Mayers and Jeffrey Zoul.
Other titles: Ten perspectives on equity in education
Description: First Edition. | New York : Routledge, 2021. |
Series: Great Educators Series | Includes bibliographical references. |
Identifiers: LCCN 2021001731 (print) | LCCN 2021001732 (ebook) |
ISBN 9780367553555 (Hardback) | ISBN 9780367553531 (Paperback) |
ISBN 9781003093145 (eBook)
Subjects: LCSH: Educational equalization. | Educational change. |
Discrimination in education. | Critical pedagogy.
Classification: LCC LC213 T46 2021 (print) |
LCC LC213 (ebook) | DDC 379.2/6–dc23
LC record available at https://lccn.loc.gov/2021001731
LC ebook record available at https://lccn.loc.gov/2021001732

ISBN: 978-0-367-55355-5 (hbk)
ISBN: 978-0-367-55353-1 (pbk)
ISBN: 978-1-003-09314-5 (ebk)

Typeset in Palatino
by Newgen Publishing UK

Contents

    Racial Consciousness in Hiring Practices to
    Support Racial Equity Transformation in Schools 127
    Josh Seldess

10 Being more than "The Help" 144
    Marlena Gross-Taylor

    Afterword: It's All about Leadership 157
    Jimmy Casas

Meet the Authors

Onica L. Mayers (@O_L_Mayers) currently serves as a director for professional staffing and employee relations for human resources in the third largest school district in Texas. In her 22-year educational journey, she has served as a classroom teacher, instructional coach, assistant principal and elementary school principal for six years. Her most humbling experience was being recognized  as the 2018 Elementary Principal of the Year. Onica is currently a doctoral candidate at the University of Houston with a goal to ultimately support district and campus leaders to view their leadership through a culturally responsive lens by leading with diversity, equity and inclusion at the forefront of their thinking. She believes that being a servant leader means that you must #BeTheModel always. She shared her story in *Education Write Now, Volume II*, which she co-authored with Jeffrey Zoul et al. Onica values her professional learning network and believes in the mottos #EachOneTeachOne and #BetterTogether.

Rosa Perez-Isiah (@RosaIsiah) has served students in her community for over 26 years. Currently, she serves as director of elementary, equity and access in California. Rosa is passionate about education equity, multilingual education, leadership, and closing opportunity gaps for historically underserved students. Rosa's life experiences as an immigrant, English language learner,

and a child in poverty add to her passion for her work. Rosa is founder of the Twitter chat #WeLeadEd and the WeLeadEd BAM Radio podcast, which is focused on education leadership and social justice. Rosa co-authored three books on the whole child, equity, and the power of relationships. She contributes her voice to blogs, podcasts, and books on social justice, diversity, equity, access, and women in leadership. Rosa was the recipient of the 2019 Leader for Social Justice award from Loyola Marymount University. She is a solution tree culture and equity professional development associate. She has also presented internationally on leadership and social justice topics.

Marcie Faust (@mfaust) is an elementary school principal who is passionate about redefining educational experiences in the modern-day classroom. Prior to her role as principal, Marcie was an early childhood program director as well as a director for innovative learning. Marcie also has experience as an elementary and middle school teacher, and a technology coach. She believes in authentic, connected learning to prepare students for their futures.

Kim Hofmann (@Hofmann_Kim) graduated from the University of Notre Dame with a Bachelors degree in psychology. She went on to earn graduate degrees in school psychology and educational leadership. As a former school psychologist, Kim has extensive experience and expertise in the special education arena. Coupled with 20 years of experience in building, central office, and agency leadership in the areas of early childhood, curriculum and instruction and special populations, Kim has helped to redefine how schools deliver curriculum and supports for students. Kim's passion is working with leaders and teachers to develop and implement systemic supports to ensure all students learn at high levels. Kim has presented and consulted both regionally and at the state level, promoting and supporting schools to challenge the status quo. Kim challenges organizations to reimagine the systems and supports offered to students along the pre-K–12 educational continuum. Her mantra is inspired by Rita Pierson, "every child deserves a champion." Kim is dedicated to developing systems in schools to ensure every child has a champion.

Oman Frame has 27 years of experience in teaching and diversity leadership. He is a gifted motivator and educator who combines real-world topics with academic rigor to make learning personally meaningful for his students. Oman has conducted workshops at the National Association of Independent Schools (NAIS) People of Color Conference, the National Middle School Association Conference, and the Southern  Association of Independent Schools conference. He is a creator of curricula that ignite, motivate, and inspire people of all ages to understand the effects of oppression on underserved communities and inspire social justice commitment. Oman is currently the director of diversity, equity, and inclusion at the Paideia School in Atlanta, Georgia. He is also a member of the high school faculty. Oman is a community resource, serving as a consultant to various entities in the country. He has delivered keynotes and program content at the bell hooks Institute, Georgia Gwinnett College, and various schools and corporate institutions. He co-chaired the NAIS 2016 People of Color Conference in Atlanta, Georgia, and is also an integral part of the iChange Summer Institute for teachers. Recently Oman co-authored a book *Let's Get Real: Exploring Race, Class and Gender Identities in the Classroom*, a text that gives new life and direction to a curriculum rooted in social justice. Oman was featured in Catherine A. Corman and Edward Hallowell's *Positively ADD: Real Success Stories to Inspire Your Dreams* and was an 11Alive Class Act teacher, as well as an ION Television Everyday Hero in 2013. He is a loving husband and father, and also an active Star Wars fan.

Jeffrey Zoul (@jeff_zoul) is a lifelong teacher, learner, and leader. During Jeff's distinguished career in education he has served in a variety of roles, most recently as assistant superintendent for teaching and learning with Deerfield Public Schools District 109 in Deerfield, Illinois. Jeff also served as a teacher and coach in the state of Georgia for many years before moving into school administration. Jeff has also taught graduate courses at the university level in the areas of assessment, research, and program evaluation. Jeff has been recognized as a local Teacher of the Year and as an outstanding principal in the state of Georgia. He also served as principal at a national School of Excellence in Illinois. He is the author/co-author of more than a dozen books, including *What Connected Educators Do Differently*; *Start. Right. Now.: Teach and Lead for Excellence*; *Improving Your School One Week at a Time*; *The Principled Principal*; and *Leading Professional Learning: Tools to Connect and Empower Teachers*. Jeff has spoken at conferences and school districts in more than thirty states. He has earned several degrees, including his undergraduate degree from the University of Massachusetts and his doctoral degree from the University of Alabama. In his spare time, Jeff enjoys running and has completed over a dozen marathons. Connect with Jeff on Twitter: @jeff_zoul.

Salome Thomas-EL (@Principal_EL) lives in Pennsylvania with his family and has been a teacher and principal since 1987. He is currently the head of school at Thomas Edison Public Charter School in Wilmington, Delaware. Principal EL received national acclaim as a teacher and chess coach at Vaux Middle School, Philadelphia, where his students have gone on to win world recognition as  eight-time National Chess Champions. Principal EL was a regular contributor on the The Dr. Oz Show and is the author of the best-selling books:

> *I Choose to Stay: A Black Teacher Refuses to Desert the Inner City* (the movie rights for which were optioned by Disney Films).
> *The Immortality of Influence* (foreword by Will Smith), which stresses the importance of leadership, mentoring, parenting, and service to others.
> *Passionate Leadership: Creating a Culture of Success in Every School*, a newly released title co-authored with Joseph M. Jones and Thomas J. Vari, which deals with improving school cultures.

Thomas-EL speaks to groups around the country and frequently appears on C-SPAN, CNN, and NPR Radio. Principal EL has studied at the University of Cambridge in England, Lehigh University in Pennsylvania, and holds a doctorate in education leadership and innovation from Wilmington University in Delaware. He has received the Marcus A. Foster Award as the Outstanding School District Administrator in Philadelphia and the University of Pennsylvania's distinguished Martin Luther King Award. Educational Leadership and Reader's Digest magazines recognized Principal EL as an "Inspiring American Icon." Principal EL has also appeared on the Oprah Radio network.

Abdul Wright (@AB_Wright) is an eighth grade language arts teacher in north Minneapolis. He is also an instructional coach and data team leader. He has taught language arts for the past six years. Mr. Wright strives to make a positive difference in impoverished communities, while also striving to be the best version of himself. He completed an African American leadership program in the spring of 2016 and graduated from Hamline University with a degree in education. Mr. Wright earned his Bachelors degree in communication arts and literature in 2011. He received the Minneapolis PeaceMaker award from the city of Minneapolis in 2015, the "You've Made a Difference" award from Cristo Rey Jesuit High School in 2015 and 2016, and was the recipient of the 2016 Minnesota Teacher of the Year award. Mr. Wright was recognized as the first Black male to receive the award, and also the youngest, and the first from a charter school. In 2018, Mr. Wright was identified as a Minnesota African American Heritage Award Honoree. Abdul Wright also served a term as the board chair of the charter school The Mastery School in north Minneapolis.

Josh Seldess is currently a middle school assistant principal in Evanston, Illinois, and his 23 years in public education reflect his deep commitment to fulfilling public schools' promise to educate *all* students. Josh has also been a classroom teacher and academic department chair at the high school level, and has delivered professional development and trainings on racial equity both locally and throughout the US.

Marlena Gross-Taylor (@mgrosstaylor) is the founder of EduGladiators and a nationally recognized ed leader with a proven track record of improving educational and operational performance through vision, strategic planning, leadership, and team building. A Nashville transplant originally from southern Louisiana, Marlena's educational experience spans several states, allowing her  to have served K–12 students in both rural and urban districts. She has been recognized as a middle school master teacher and innovative administrator at the elementary, middle, high school, and district levels. Because of her sound knowledge of both elementary and secondary education, Marlena has broad-based experience creating and implementing dynamic interactive programs to attain district goals while leveraging her flexibility, resourcefulness, and organizational and interpersonal skills to foster learning through a positive, encouraging environment. As a proud Louisiana State University alumni, she is committed to excellence and believes all students can achieve. Follow Marlena on Twitter @mgrosstaylor or visit her websites: www.marlenataylor.com and www.edugladiators.com.

Jimmy Casas (@casas_jimmy) served 22 years as a school leader, including 14 years as principal at Bettendorf High School in Bettendorf, Iowa. Under his leadership, Bettendorf was named one of the "Best High Schools" in the country three times by *Newsweek* and *US News & World Report*. Jimmy was named the 2012 Iowa Secondary Principal of the Year and was selected by the National Association  of Secondary School Principals as one of three finalists for their 2013 National Secondary Principal of the Year award . In 2014, Jimmy was invited to the White House to speak on the Future Ready Schools® pledge. Jimmy is also the author/co-author of six books, *What Connected Educators Do Differently*; *Start. Right. Now.: Teach and Lead for Excellence*; the best-selling book *Culturize – Every Student. Every Day. Whatever it Takes*; *Stop. Right. Now.: The 39 Stops to Making Schools Better*; *Live Your Excellence: Bring Your Best Self to School Every Day*; and his latest release, *Daily Inspiration for Educators: Positive Thoughts for Every Day of the Year*. Finally, Jimmy is the owner and CEO of J Casas & Associates, an educational leadership company aimed at organizing and providing world-class professional coaching and learning services for educators across the country.

Introduction

About the Routledge *Great Educators Series* Books

In 2015, Jeffrey Zoul, Jimmy Casas, and Todd Whitaker decided to organize a new type of professional learning conference for educators serving in any role, from classroom teacher to superintendent, and everything in between. They eventually created ConnectEDD (www.connectEDD.org) as an organization dedicated to inspiring and motivating educators everywhere to innovate, experiment, and connect with each other to become the very best they can be as professional educators. The first *What Great Educators Do Differently* (WGEDD) conference was held in the Chicago area in the fall of 2015. Jeff, Jimmy, and Todd reached out to some of the best educators they knew and asked them to share their wisdom over the course of the two-day event. This inaugural conference was so successful, that they continued hosting events. Since that time, they have hosted more than twenty additional events in ten different states as well as Canada.

In addition to the professional learning events hosted by ConnectEDD, an idea for a collaborative book series was hatched. Routledge was excited to partner with these educational authors to create a different kind of book, one we hope captures the spirit of WGEDD events and provides diverse insights into important topics facing educators. Each year, ten authors write a chapter loosely focused on an overall theme to help educators continue their learning.

Launching Volume I: All About Innovation

We began the series in 2019 with the theme of *Innovation in Education*. We were honored that the following educators agreed to support this book by contributing their thoughts on some aspect of education and how we can become more innovative in the ways we think about and approach that part of our work as professional educators: Jeffrey Zoul, Todd Whitaker, Jimmy Casas, Thomas C. Murray, Starr Sackstein, Kirk Humphreys, Shannon McClintock Miller, Katrina Keene, Dwight Carter, and LaVonna Roth. Topics included in Volume I ranged from innovative professional learning, to innovative hiring practices, to innovative learning spaces, to innovative math classrooms.

Launching Volume II: All About Learning

We continued the series in 2020 by inviting ten educators to weigh in on the broad theme of *Learning*. We are honored that the following educators agreed to support this book by contributing their thoughts on some aspect of learning in our classrooms, schools, and districts today: Todd Whitaker, Jeffrey Zoul, Jimmy Casas, Sanée Bell, Garnet Hillman, Kayla Dornfeld, Jessica Cabeen, Brian Mendler, Erin Klein, and Derek McCoy. Topics included in Volume II ranged from learning to lead to nonnegotiables for success in reaching our hardest-to-reach kids, to "unlearning" traditional practices that are no longer effective, to creating student-centered learning environments.

Launching Volume III: Equity Issues in Education

We continue the series, of course, with the volume you are reading now. In this volume, we reached out to educators who have presented at WGEDD events as well as other educators we respect to weigh in on a topic that is timely, important, and urgent: Equity. We are honored that the following educators agreed to support this book project by contributing their thoughts on some aspect of educational equity facing our classrooms, schools, districts, and the educators who serve therein. Although the chapters touch on a variety of equity issues, a recurring theme is that, at its core, "equity" is all about giving every child what that child needs to succeed. Here, then, are the ten authors of Volume III of the Great Educators book series:

Onica L. Mayers (@O_L_Mayers) examines the importance of equity through a human resources lens, suggesting that attracting, advancing, and retaining diverse talent to better meet the needs of our diverse customers—our students and their families—is our responsibility as educators. She discusses how we can adopt an equity mindset, create an equity plan and use it to drive our actions, and expand our equity vision by supporting, listening, persisting—and disrupting the status quo.

Rosa Perez-Isiah (@RosaIsiah) takes a look at the diverse cultural and linguistic experiences and knowledge that many of our students bring to the schoolhouse which are often perceived to be deficits that require rectification, when, in fact, they are strengths and funds of knowledge that contribute greatly to learning. Embracing a student's cultural capital plays a vital role in the academic identity and success of students of color. Isiah shares strategies that will support educators seeking to acknowledge and tap into the strengths that students of color bring to school as they work to provide them with access, equity, and high levels of learning, while resisting a historically oppressive system of education for many.

Marcie Faust (@mfaust) offers specific ideas for breaking down barriers that prevent all children from participating in early childhood programs that support their development and ensures school readiness. Faust believes that embracing inclusivity and diversity among young students is the professional obligation of all early childhood professionals and she explores ways to advance equity in early childhood education, to address biases, reflect on current practices, and design programs and opportunities to help all young children reach their full potential.

Kim Hofmann (@Hofmann_Kim) suggests that some of our students often have limited access to educational opportunities they need in order to succeed. She identifies three "barriers" that traditionally limit such access—our beliefs, our schedules, and our systems—and for each of these barriers, offers "opportunities" for overcoming them. She challenges educators not to become complacent when it comes to educational disparities that exist and not to continue to operate as they always have simply because that is how it has always been done.

Oman Frame takes a deep dive into the concept of intersectional identity and the way systemic and individual oppression impact our interpretation of every moment we spend in community. He begins the process of unpacking the multiple and dynamic identities that make up our experiences, as well as how those identities together create our worldview. Frame suggests that an intersectional approach allows the community to validate the whole person and keep the focus on certain aspects of our social world. He also suggests that intersectional work is the next phase of truly inclusive classrooms. By understanding the multidimensional and multilayered students in front of us, we are able to tailor lessons designed for students' internal knowledge of themselves.

Jeffrey Zoul (@jeff_zoul) makes a case for more equitable assessment practices in our schools. Many of the traditional grading and assessment practices we have clung to in schools for far too long are irrelevant or even counterproductive to student learning. Worse still, many of these practices serve as barriers to ensuring equity. Ensuring that every student gets what they need when it comes to grading and assessment is an urgent and important teaching and learning matter. To achieve equity in terms of grading and assessment, we must shift the way we think about many of our current practices. Zoul looks at how we can rethink competition, tracking, and enrichment programs, and practice and feedback, shifting from systems that sort students into "winners" and "losers" to systems that level the playing field for all students, ensuring that each child is provided with what they need to succeed.

Salome Thomas-EL (@Principal_EL) shares his wisdom about building resilience, critical thinking skills, and problem-solving capabilities within students from all backgrounds. He suggests that one way to provide more opportunities for instilling these success traits within all students is by offering after-school programs for all students. He specifically shares his passion for the game of chess and how it has positively impacted scores of students at schools where he has served for many years. According to Thomas-EL, the education of our students will be their saving grace, so we must ensure that all students receive the very best opportunities possible. Building resilience through chess has been a great equalizer among the student populations Salome has served, becoming a game changer in terms of more equitable educational outcomes.

Abdul Wright (@AB_Wright) tackles the idea that at any time in society, one of two cultures is prevalent: A culture of competition or a culture of cooperation. He argues that we need to abolish the former and work to enact the latter. Wright shares his personal journey growing up and how it has impacted his thinking today, leading him to believe that equity is simply "actionable hope." When people have genuine hope, they not only recognize the vision and mission, which is to give all people an opportunity to have quality in all facets of their life, but to also feel a sense of belonging and connectedness to this mission of seeing all people, especially young people who have been marginalized, oppressed and/or silenced, regain a sense of identity, belonging, and purpose that all people deserve.

Josh Seldess provides an honest look at hiring practices in schools through an equity lens, suggesting that schools have a moral obligation to hire and retain a racially diverse workforce. He offers five key concepts towards deepening racial consciousness around your school's hiring practices that

support the broader work of systemic racial equity transformation in schools. Seldess argues that making sure we
have racially conscious educators, and effective processes
for hiring them, is one small, but important, step toward
institutional racial equity transformation.

Marlena Gross-Taylor (@mgrosstaylor) shares her belief that
in order to eradicate the barriers Black Americans have had
to endure specifically around occupational hierarchy, we
have to start with a systemic approach to increase stake-
holder commitment to racial equity coupled with intentional actions that truly value and support a culture rooted
in equity and diversity. She shares three critical pillars to
begin the work of eradicating occupational barriers facing
our students (awareness, action, and reflection), explaining
how each can help us move forward to a more equitable
system for all.

Jimmy Casas.(@casas_jimmy) closes this volume by focusing
on leadership, making the case that, absent of strong school
leadership, we will never achieve the level of success we
need when it comes to creating more equitable schools.
Casas argues that effecting change of any kind in our
schools—or our society at large—requires strong leaders
and strong leadership. Achieving equity in our schools is
all about leadership. And it simply cannot happen if only
some of us lead. The issue of equity is too important—and,
in fact, too daunting—to think it will happen unless each of
us plays an active leadership role in promoting and, eventually, achieving it.

We hope you had the opportunity to read the first two volumes of
the Routledge *Great Educators Series* and we are thankful you are
reading Volume III. Please share your thoughts and contribute
to the discussion on Twitter, using the #10Perspectives hashtag
when you do. We are biased, of course, but we believe that education is the most important profession imaginable. What we
do as educators matters, and it matters every day. We cannot
afford to settle for the status quo in our work when we know a
better way. When we know better, we must do better. Although

we must always do the things we do better, we must also do new and better things in our classrooms, schools, and districts. Continuously doing new and better things is how we can eventually achieve equity in our classrooms, schools, and districts. Thank you for reading this book, sharing your thoughts—and continuing to learn in your role as an educator.

1

Equity in Education
The Underlying Impact—Recruitment to Retention

Onica L. Mayers

Equity Defined

Equity does not mean the same thing to every organization. Having a common language is important in establishing a baseline for diversity, equity and inclusion (DEI) work. The baseline for diversity relates to backgrounds and perspectives; inclusion relates to equal rate, belonging, allowed to contribute. Fundamentally they bleed into each other but organizationally they have different implications based on the organizational structure.

When you hear the word "equity", what is the first thing that comes to mind? Don't think long and hard…what is your first thought? Some thoughts shared on this perspective were:

♦ Determining who needs what to be successful, by providing all that they need, how they need it, and in a way that they are able to receive it so we can learn from those needs and use this knowledge in the future.

◆ Giving people what *they* need to succeed, which is the opposite of equality. Equity would not allow for a cookie cutter or one-size-fits-all model, but would remain cognizant of who is actually determining what it is that people actually need, absent of the determining person's perception or privilege.

◆ Giving each person what they need in that moment to be successful, which requires having the right mindset and being purposeful in action and reflection.

The common thread to note is an emphasis on individual success. The mere task of defining the word "equity" is in itself a challenge. Just as no two schools or students are the same, no two people are going to define equity using the same words, however, it is the hope that the connotation of what equity stands for in education that has common threads interwoven. Equity work for all intents and purposes must not be considered ad hoc; to the contrary, it should be the centerpiece of what we do, and the why behind what we do. A true commitment to equitable education will require that all stakeholders in the process recognize that, in fact, it is a process, one that is a marathon and not a sprint, and undoubtedly not a box to be checked. But, by all means, there is an end in sight, even when running a marathon. We insult those in the underrepresented groups when we know that we have organizations that systematically shut them out and we are somehow content with taking a long period of time to help resolve inadequacies.

For me, a former classroom teacher, instructional coach, assistant principal, elementary school principal, and now director of human resources, equity is being aware of unconscious bias, beginning with hiring diverse talent, and moving beyond that to creating experiences and environments, schools included, that shape whether people—staff and students—remain and thrive.

"Systemic equity [exists when]…systems and individuals habitually operate to ensure that every student has the greatest opportunity to learn, enhanced by the resources and supports necessary to achieve competence, excellence, independence, personal and social responsibility, and self sufficiency for school and for life" (Bradley, 2000). That said, we know that the most important factor in ensuring systemic equity exists for students daily is the teacher in the classroom.

Equity moves the needle beyond arbitrary status hierarchies where status differences are solely based on what someone happens to be born as, rather than their competence or ability. An equity-centered approach is responsive to the cultural identities of students, staff and the community served. We would be derelict in our responsibilities if we did not reflect on our culturally responsive practices and ensure that our students can see themselves reflected in the staff and leadership, as well as their backgrounds, languages, culture and learning styles incorporated in the curriculum. We must work to reduce cultural misunderstandings and deepen our knowledge of understanding the diversity of belief systems and values in the communities we serve.

Do We Have an Equity Issue in Schools?

Bill de la Cruz shared that brick and mortar schools as we know them in the traditional sense were designed to educate a homogenous group of students; a homogenous group of White students in a system based on equality versus equity (cited in Snyder, Trowery & McGrath, 2019). That system not only centered around a mostly White population of students, but also around a White population of men as the educators. Today, we are at the crossroads of attempting to modify the system as we know it to be equity focused, equity as it aligns to supporting the diverse needs of students and those who teach them, as well as the inclusive environments for both groups as well. This reckoning requires transparency supported with action. This is where we are now, and what are we going to do about it?

To meet the moment, we have to be stronger than our excuses. A review of the traditional design of schools will uncover that DEI practices are undermined. Many would agree that equity or inequity in education is perhaps the primary civil rights issue of our time. And can we truly discuss equity without reframing our current standards to include *diversity*, **equity** and *inclusion*? The inequities in education have been evident for generations, yet today, as the rubber meets the road, we can no longer maintain the unsatisfactory status quo. If not now, when?

Adopting an equity mindset is paramount to the success of any organization's attempt at transformational change, and schools are not exempt. The *Guiding Principles for Equity Education* emphasized that, "striving for equity often requires fundamental structural changes that go beyond temporary initiatives or surface-level changes" (Snyder, Trowery & McGrath, 2019). What we are facing today is the stark reality that if we do not work together to address the need for equitable education, we could potentially widen the gap before we narrow it.

Recruitment to Retention

In our realm of education, diversification of the workforce through the organization hierarchy is attainable. We must intentionally promote the full engagement of diverse employees by facilitating experiences of belonging, being valued for one's uniqueness. We cannot simply hire based on algorithmic hiring methods that perpetuate inherent biases. It starts with recruiters and hiring managers having sensitivity training.

Attracting, advancing and retaining diverse talent to better meet the needs of our diverse customers—our students and their families—is our responsibility as school leaders. But it begs the question, are the recruitment efforts aligned with this goal? It goes without saying, or maybe not, perhaps it is not as crystalized as it needs to be—that we should embrace and truly encourage all of our employees' differences, including personalities, values, passions and personal interests which highlight their uniqueness.

To create such experiences and environments requires having the right people in the right places, from leadership to support staff. This requires work, and equity work must be seen through a lens in which all decisions are made. It begins with recruitment efforts which might mean that the manner in which we hire teachers, campus leaders and central office administrators must change. And yes, change is a constant, but in education, change is not so readily embraced. How do we begin the paradigm shift to embrace the changes needed to restructure our hiring processes?

Hiring with DEI in mind begins with the leadership of the organization asking if there are current diversity goals, and subsequently, if the current hiring processes reflect a commitment to ensuring that the measurable outcomes are met. DEI leaders need to and must be empowered by those at the helm, and those leaders must be aware of their own unconscious biases.

It goes without saying that if the organization does not have such goals, implementing them is a necessary first step in ensuring that staff members—teachers, support staff, administrators (and extended to the selection of board members)—are viewed through a DEI lens. Perhaps if we had the opportunity to peel back the layers of the onion even further, the question that would lay the foundation would be: Does the leadership of the organization recognize that there is a need to have DEI goals and are those goals ultimately supported by a hiring process that aims to achieve them? Thus, depending on how many layers you are peeling back, therein lies your starting point. If our goal is to ascertain the root cause, one could also go beyond the K–12 realm and delve into the student teacher pipeline that is generated at the tertiary level, for that is where recruitment originates.

In the absence of DEI goals, the organization should consider a thorough, transparent, and reflective equity audit process. Dr. Roger Cleveland, who received the P.G. Peeples Equity and Excellence Achievement Award from the Fayette County Equity Council for his work in improving local schools, uses discovery conversations with the board and district's leadership to begin the process of conducting an equity and culture audit. Can you work on a problem that has yet to be identified as such? As educators, we all know that what is monitored and measured matters, and without the support of the head of the organization, DEI work will not infiltrate schools and departments across a district and impact the intended beneficiaries—students. Discovery conversations followed by surveying stakeholders (including students, teaching and non-teaching staff, parents, and administrators), an extensive data review, as well as "boots on the ground" campus visits, all lead to the development of an equity policy. With the creation of an equity policy, all staff members, existing and new staff as they are onboarded, must receive professional development to have a thorough understanding of the district's expectations and equity policies. This process is the genesis of the acquisition of an equity mindset which will in turn support the work needed to drive your equity plan forward and expand the vision of the organization with DEI work as its foundation.

Operating on the assumption that the school district has established equity goals, a critical self-reflection question is this: Are you seeking to hire candidates who will bring value to the diverse perspectives of the given community? More specifically, are the potential teachers, support staff members and administrators representative of those who have been intentionally or unintentionally underrepresented and/or marginalized in the educational organization? Clear articulation of this question as the overall mission of the campus or district must be conveyed by the person overseeing the hiring process.

The hiring committee itself should be reflective of the diversity of perspectives that the organization values, and they should be prepared to ask candidates about their understanding and experience with DEI work in the quest for equity warriors. This will highlight candidates' commitments or lack thereof as you strive to have people on board who have an equity purpose; for these are the people who can and will inspire and prepare our students for the unchartered territory that lies ahead.

These change agents will be the ones in our organizations to determine the learning outcomes for our students and their opportunities moving forward. The committee should agree on their "look-fors" as it pertains to a candidate's understanding of the role social justice plays in education, why the candidate truly wants to serve in the capacity being sought in that specific campus/district/department, and be able to articulate his/her philosophy on traditional education and the corrections that can be made to ensure equity in education. Don't hesitate to share your educational values and the direction in which the organization is heading. These should not be kept in the vault.

How do we set up employees to be successful? In an effort to better meet the needs of our students, we, the leadership of the campus/district, must remain steadfast and consistent in ensuring that ongoing meaningful and relevant formal and informal professional development is provided to the staff. This does not have to be an intricate task, and can be a series of facilitated discussions. Open discourse may test the waters of the organization, but weighing the risk of silence versus the reward of understanding…you be the judge. As the educators and leaders embrace the conversations around DEI, they can steer the students entrusted to their care toward a safe learning environment rather than having their voices unheard, or worse, stifled. Support teachers as they engage and continue to build relationships with students in innovative ways.

Targeted mentoring, support navigating through the social side of the organization outside of the formal structure, while also getting the formal skills needed to advance within the organization all impact retention. In essence, what is required is a holistic integrated experience for all employees.

In conjunction with continued growth and development opportunities for teachers, it is imperative that leaders are supported to be able to coach teachers and network with others doing DEI work. In *Principals Need Help Building Anti-Racist Schools*, Superville noted:

> It [building anti-racist schools] takes time and it has to be repeated—over and over. It's uncomfortable—both for the principal who may be examining his/her own identity for the first time, and the teachers and staff who're going to be asked to do so. And there will be pushback, especially from those who see the world through race-neutral lenses or are wedded to colorblindness. People may leave. They may think that the principal who is asking them to think critically about race (and equity) is the one being divisive.
>
> Superville (2020)

The human brain is wired for survival. Employees with a homogenous lifestyle who are not accustomed to being uncomfortable will feel threatened with DEI work.

This newfound relationship would allow both teachers and students, administrators and teachers, to begin to tear down walls leading to the rebuilding of a new foundation built on norms and agreements that allow for active engagement despite the possible uncomfortable experiences. What this provides is opportunities for everyone to speak their truth and repressed emotions to be safely released. Consider creating a safe space using listening tours to give employees pockets of opportunities. You must, must, must get into the psychology of making people feel more secure. There is no escaping frank conversations; honesty is missing from failed equity-minded efforts.

Soliciting feedback from all stakeholders cannot be seen as optional. Align practices with performance data. It is indeed a required element in cementing an equity vision for a campus, department or district. This vision needs to be a roadmap that includes the common language to be used, leaving no room for misinterpretation—it has to be intentional. Identifying and clearly communicating agreed upon goals that are research based and data driven is non-negotiable.

The Work of Equity-Centered Leaders

It is imperative that you follow through on the integration of DEI efforts; integration is not synonymous with a one-day, one-off training. Prepare an integrated set of processes and practices, not a single initiative, with established evaluation, support, development and measurable objectives. Data must effectively measure the initiative and know that just as with good teaching, one measures, calibrates and adjusts along the way, using the data to isolate where the challenges are. In this process, we cannot neglect soft skills, those emotional intelligences that can be raw emotions captured in quantifiable data. Be willing to dig in and use tools to layer insight.

Translate the data collected over time into a narrative so that leadership can make strategic change. Do not shortchange the process—measure your DEI efforts and their retention impact. Although we know that equity in education leads to higher teacher and student performance, we still have not moved the needle as significantly as needed, so we have to monitor and adjust, and open up the emotional side.

The not-so-good data is also important to chew on. When those who are reflective of the DEI efforts leave the organization, sometimes at a rate of 2:1, you may ask yourself, where do you begin? Work to understand the *why* through authentic exit interviews, but more importantly, talk to people while they are still members of the organization. Don't make assumptions which may lead you to try to solve the "wrong" problem. Be intentional with creating relationships when times are good, so that people feel comfortable coming to express their thoughts when times are not so good.

As a society, could we overcome tribalism by simply the reporting of its statistical data? Encourage and support the unification around the mission and vision of the organization and people will inherently make an emotional transition. While data is necessary, it is not sufficient. The evidence should be visible in student achievement data, discipline data, staff hiring needs, and community impact. Start small, but start, and the long-term commitment to DEI work is a barometer by which oneself can be measured.

…To Better Serve Our Students

What is the school's and/or district's mission? Do all stakeholders know it? Believe it? Live it? If it in any way pertains to students being global, forward thinkers, then we are obligated to further our efforts to create an equitable, diverse and inclusive environment in schools that directly align to the said mission. Students may be the ones leading the way, as they are typically better at engaging in conversations about equity and their inherent needs. As such, they need in their corner educators who understand their needs and deserve to be part of school communities with comprehensive, equitable systems, prepared to navigate the barriers to teaching and learning.

Let's be clear and avoid sugarcoating the issue. Equity in education sparks conflict and controversy, and when it does not, the deafening silence is voluminous. What should be expected is that the courageous conversations required to avoid the fall into silence will lead to discomfort. When we take the "un" out of uncomfortable, that is how we begin to lay the foundation of meaningful change in schools and organizations as a whole. Note that the pit in our stomach that arises with an uncomfortable conversation is telling about our own experiences and perspectives, along with that of others—others who may not be like ourselves. This is where and how we begin the abandonment of old habits.

We cannot truly serve our students' best interests without identifying the dimensions of equity that matter most in our society and in our respective institutions and without thinking about any organizational disruptors that may also exist.

Begin by identifying what current happenings are taking place globally, nationally and most importantly locally. This consideration of the sociohistorical landscape will shed light on those in your educational setting who have access to people in decision-making positions. Demonstrate a willingness to reflect upon your organizational structure, culture and climate, and identify who, in terms of equity, enjoys the greater privilege and who has the capacity to disrupt the unspoken norms. Address issues head on, and make sure that employees know what is being addressed, why, and how. Open lines of communication without repercussions will truly provide an opportunity to garner the essence of the culture.

Check Your Privilege

To understand the impact of DEI in our educational institutions, we must understand systems of privilege. If you were to check your privilege, you may recognize that there are indeed privileges that you enjoy within the workplace that you may not even be aware of. Some of us are more privileged than others. Take note of how your privilege is impacting how you support students, staff, and families. If you were to examine your work environment, what would you notice about who holds the power and the authority? If you are the one yielding the authority, what do others notice about you? Leaders must model their own learning and be willing to acknowledge their privilege, biases and fears if they are going to help others overcome theirs and be willing to take risks in exploring and sharing in this growth process.

Structures of power as well as influence have an impact on our daily interaction with others. We all need to look in the mirror to develop an awareness of the social identity groups to which we belong and note how that leads to higher status in our society and affords privilege with or without knowing.

There are segments of our organizations that have certain groups under- or overrepresented. What does that mean in terms of equity in your organization? Perhaps homegrown or internal employees have more privilege in your organization than a mid-career hire. As you hire and map out your retention efforts with DEI in mind, be aware that the more balanced the workforce demographics of an organization throughout all levels—support staff, professional staff, administrators—the less likely it is for one social identity category to automatically have that unyielding greater status, i.e. privilege.

This! Privilege is an invisible package of unearned assets which one can count on cashing in daily and to which the person is oblivious. Dr. Peggy McIntosh, anti-racism activist and scholar, hit the nail on the head in unpacking that invisible knapsack of White privilege.

Understanding what is concealed in your invisible backpack is a journey into enlightenment. Start with a belief in equality, recognize that belief is not enough and the paradigm shift will transition organically to recognizing that in our organizations, equity means that we provide the support that *we* believe others need. Ultimately, we listen to *their voice* and offer a seat at the table.

Be *the* Disruptor

Lead with vulnerability and begin with the understanding that we are engineered to be where we have been and it is due time for processes to be reengineered to be more inclusive. Disparities did not occur by happenstance. We have to begin by educating stakeholders on how we arrived at this point. Assume nothing; assumptions create emotions.

As you process and internalize and identify your own growth opportunities in moving your campus/department/organization to create more equitable experiences, you can be an intentional steward, a disruptor of sorts. You can be the one to make the necessary changes, shake things up. You, *the* disruptor, can support the evolution of creating new ways of behaving, acting and doing, and interrupt that status quo and force those with whom you serve into new ways of behaving. Be willing to be aggressive within the walls of the organization but look beyond your four walls as well. Disrupt the patterns that alienate or disempower families of those who have been underserved or marginalized and empower and value them.

In *Beginning Courageous Conversations about Race*, Singleton and Hays (2008) identify discussion questions which, if you replace "race" with "equity", can yield quite insightful thoughts:

- ◆ Why might educators find talking about race (*equity*) particularly important?
- ◆ If you have had—or tried to have—conversations about race (*equity*) with your colleagues, or with your students, what happened? If you have not, describe a time you wish you had, and what stopped you from initiating or participating fully in the conversation.
- ◆ If you were to start a conversation about some race (*equity*) issue with your colleagues, what issue would you like it to be?

Disruptors are willing to take steps to recognize unconscious bias and how it impacts the way people perceive, assess, and react to their peers. Now that you have an awareness of your own unconscious bias, look at your campus/district/department through bias-stained glasses. Are there unconscious biases that may have existed without you even noticing them? Please recognize that unconscious bias, mine and yours, is not a negative reflection or criticism of us as employees or the organization. We all have those thoughts that pop into our heads. It isn't so much the thought that creeps into your psyche that is the problem, but the actions you take after the thought manifests itself. Be prepared to battle your unconscious bias if you truly want to look in the mirror and say, "Change begins with me."

Do yourself a favor and set the right benchmark. Don't necessarily compare yourselves to others in your organization/district to benchmark where you are. Simply ask yourself:

◆ What do I want my campus/department/district to look like?
◆ What do we want our culture to be?
◆ What do we want it to feel like for someone in an underrepresented group to work here?

The *Guiding Principles for Equity in Education* (Snyder, Trowery & McGrath, 2019) can launch you into your DEI work:

◆ Adopt an equity mindset.
  ◆ *Commit*: Understand that equity is a journey that requires collaborative commitments.
  ◆ *Collaborate*: Value and prioritize inclusive communication.
  ◆ *Frame*: Foster a culture that encourages self-reflection and new perspectives.
◆ Drive your equity plan.
  ◆ *Nurture*: Provide social and emotional supports to all students and staff.
  ◆ *Empathize*: Implement culturally responsive teaching practices.
  ◆ *Build*: Replace institutional inequities with innovative supports.

- ◆ *Challenge*: Ensure that all students are held to high expectations.
- ◆ Expand your equity vision.
  - ◆ *Support*: Deliver ongoing professional learning opportunities.
  - ◆ *Listen*: Continually solicit feedback.
  - ◆ *Persist*: Drive positive change through perseverance.

School leadership is of central importance for the experience created in schools and across districts. Effective leaders *are* disruptors.

Resources

Agovino, T. (2020). We're Talking About Racism. We Never Talked About This Before. *HR Magazine*, 32–9.

Cleveland, R. (n.d.). Equity and Cultural Audits. *Millennium Learning Concepts*. Retrieved November 21, 2020, from www.millenniumlearningconcepts.org/.

McIntosh, P. (1988). *White Privilege and Male Privilege: A Personal Account of Coming To See Correspondences through Work in Women's Studies*. Excerpted from Working Paper 189. Retrieved from www.racialequitytools.org/resourcefiles/mcintosh.pdf.

Scott, B. (2000, February). We Should Not Kid Ourselves: Excellence Requires Equity. *IDRA Newsletter*. San Antonio, Texas: Intercultural Development Research Association.

Singleton, G. and Hays, C. (2008). *Beginning Courageous Conversations about Race*. Retrieved from www.courts.ca.gov/documents/BTB_23_PRECON_Make_It_Plain_2.pdf.

Snyder, A. Trowery, L. and McGrath, K. (2019, July). *Guiding Principles for Equity in Education*. Retrieved from https://medium.com/inspired-ideas-prek-12/guiding-principles-for-equity-in-education-3b8b8c22063c.

Superville, D.R. (2020, September). Principals Need Help Building Anti-Racist Schools. *Education Week*. Retrieved from www.edweek.org/ew/articles/2020/09/23/principals-need-help-building-anti-racist-schools.html.

2

Funds of Knowledge
Embracing the Cultural Capital of Students of Color

Rosa Perez-Isiah

It is hard to argue that we are teaching the whole child when school policy dictates that students leave their language and culture at the schoolhouse door.

Cummins et al. (2005)

Do you believe that students and their families have something to contribute to learning before they ever enter our classrooms? Let me rephrase that…do you believe that *students of color* and families with diverse languages and cultures have something to contribute to learning before they ever enter our classrooms? Do you believe that home language, culture, and life experiences are relevant even when they differ from yours? You might not have ever considered these perspectives, but our biases, assumptions, and beliefs about the language and culture of our students greatly influence our behaviors and learning expectations in our classrooms. The diverse cultural and linguistic experiences and knowledge that many of our students bring to the schoolhouse are often perceived to be deficits that require rectification, as the Cummins et al. (2005) quote says, when in fact, they are strengths and funds of knowledge that contribute greatly to learning. Embracing a student's cultural capital plays a vital role in the academic identity and success of students of color.

In this chapter we will explore and learn more about *funds of knowledge* and *cultural capital*, and the impact on student achievement. I will share strategies that will support educators seeking to acknowledge and tap into the strengths that students of color bring to school as they work to provide them with access, equity, and high levels of learning, while resisting a historically oppressive system of education for many.

My Funds of Knowledge Story

I identify as a Latina, a woman of color, an immigrant and an English language learner. My identity also includes the person I'm becoming…an educational leader, an advocate for social justice, and an agent for educational change. My story of becoming is deeply impacted by my culture and language, and how I was perceived as a newcomer in America many years ago.

Coming to this country was one of the most challenging things I experienced as a young child. I don't believe most people understand how distressing this experience can be for children who are attempting to adapt to a new way of being. Children are resilient and many can easily adapt to the demands of immersion, but the cost is high. The cost too often includes the loss of a student's culture and language as they struggle to assimilate.

Throughout my journey of assimilation as a young student I felt invisible and insignificant in my new community and school. I was immersed in a new language, new people, new foods, and a community unlike the one I left behind. My teachers, for the most part, were very kind. They were friendly and smiled often, attempting to engage me. It helped, but I didn't feel I had much to contribute in class and usually kept to myself. After a few negative experiences with my primary teachers, I wondered if my teachers felt the same way about me. Did they feel I had anything to contribute?

My schooling memories include a teacher looking at me and shaking her head in frustration because I couldn't master the multiplication "drill and kill" tests. I recall desperately wanting to please her with better scores, but timed tests made me nervous and I struggled to memorize math facts. I did, however, understand the concept of multiplication. What my teacher did not realize is that I went grocery shopping with my mom weekly. Not only did I translate for her whenever needed, but I was great at figuring out discounts and sale prices. The math concepts were all around me and they made much more sense to me than memorizing a bunch of math facts. These math skills and translation skills were part of my social capital and funds of knowledge as a child of color, a language learner, and a newcomer to America.

Meaningful connections and strong relationships are the foundation for learning. When students feel that we understand who they are and that we authentically care, they take emotional risks and they open their hearts and minds to connecting and learning. Relationships matter.

Relationships and Connections

The questions I asked at the beginning of this chapter were questions I wished my teachers asked of themselves when I was their newcomer student who was a learner of English. I wanted them to understand who I was, how much I loved learning and growing as an emerging multilingual student, and how much my language, culture and experiences meant to me. Early in my career as an American scholar, one teacher did.

I immigrated from Mexico as a four year old. I was too old for preschool but soon after I arrived I enrolled in kindergarten where I was completely immersed in the English language. That year was a blur for me…I was in culture shock. Things began to make sense for me in first grade. Mrs. De La Peña, my first grade teacher, changed my entire life's trajectory that year. She was one of a handful of teachers in my life that looked and sounded like me. Mrs. De La Peña was bilingual and a woman of color. She had an incredible collection of books that included books in Spanish, bilingual books, and multicultural literature with Latinx characters. Listening to her read was something I looked forward to every day. What made Mrs. De La Peña great was the time she took to get to know me, to connect with me, and to reach out to my family. She learned all about my experiences coming to America. She connected with my mother and she taught me to read in Spanish, my first language, after our full days of English immersion instruction. She gave my mother materials and books that allowed me to practice reading in both English and Spanish at home. My parents were extremely proud that their little girl was learning and developing into an emerging multilingual student.

Mrs. De La Peña understood how important relationships and connections were to my learning. She understood that affirming my home language and culture and building proficiency in both languages would translate into growth across all content areas. Mrs. De La Peña tapped into my funds of knowledge and cultural capital and made me believe that I could learn anything.

Building connections and relationships with students is the most important work a teacher can do as they engage in academic instruction. It sets the student and teacher up for great teaching and learning experiences. John Hattie shares with us that constructive teacher–student relationships have a strong and positive impact on a student's academic results. He states:

> It is teachers […] who have created positive teacher student relationships that are more likely to have the above average effects on student achievement.
>
> John Hattie (2009)

A teacher who builds positive student–teacher relationships is a teacher who seeks to understand and acknowledge her student's funds of knowledge and cultural capital. Mrs. De La Peña was my *funds of knowledge* teacher. I'm grateful to her for positively influencing my learning and my life.

Funds of Knowledge and Cultural Capital

Funds of Knowledge

I learned about funds of knowledge from the work of Norma González, author and researcher who believed that tapping into the community's funds of knowledge strengthens the home and school connection. The concept is based on a simple premise: People are competent, they have knowledge, and their life experiences have given them that knowledge. Norma and her research team believed that the connections between school and home foster *confianza* or *trust* between the two (González, Moll & Amanti, 2005). This *confianza* ultimately results in the development of healthy relationships and student achievement.

Colette Bennett shares with us that:

> The phrase fund of knowledge [...] suggests that students have knowledge assets and that these assets have been gained through authentic personal experiences. These authentic experiences can be a powerful form of learning when compared to learning through telling by as is traditionally experienced in a class. These funds of knowledge, developed in authentic experiences, are assets that can be exploited by educators for learning in the classroom.
>
> Bennett (2020)

Some key ideas to remember about the importance and value of funds of knowledge shared by Bennett (2020) include the following:

- Families have abundant knowledge that programs can learn and use in their family engagement efforts.
- Students bring with them funds of knowledge from their homes and communities that can be used for concept and skill development.
- Classroom practices sometimes underestimate and constrain what children are able to display intellectually.

Cultural Capital

A concept that is aligned with funds of knowledge is a critical race theory concept that challenges the idea that households and communities of color are deficient: Cultural capital. The cultural capital concept was explored by Dr. Tara Yosso, a researcher, educator, and author.

Dr. Yosso believed that:

> Community cultural wealth offers a more expanded view of thinking about the resources and knowledge that students of color bring to the classroom. Yosso describes community cultural wealth as a way to think about the knowledge, resources, skills, and abilities students bring to the classroom. Many times specific knowledge is valued in a family context but not in the school context.
>
> Yosso (2005)

For example, a student who translates documents for her parents who do not speak English and assists them with transactions at stores among other tasks goes to school only to find that in the school context her knowledge of two languages is not as valuable. In addition, Yosso also identifies a total of six additional types of capital that are fostered by communities of color and contribute to a community's cultural wealth. It's important that educators are aware of this capital in addition to *cultural capital.* The six types of capital are:

- **Aspirational capital**: Yosso describes this as resiliency that many develop as a result of encountering numerous barriers. Aspirational capital is about persistence in the face of repeated adversity and inequity.
- **Familial capital**: This capital is about a person's ability to connect with his/her community's success, whether they are blood related or not.
- **Linguistic capital**: This includes the capital that is obtained through the learning and sharing of multiple languages.

Social capital: The capital that networks people and resources in the community, as well as an individual's ability to join and become a member of those social networks.

Resistant capital: Resistant capital, the capital which students of color come to depend on when facing academic and social obstacles, is the ability to handle microaggressions.

Navigational capital: Yosso cites the ability of students to navigate the system they're engaged in despite the ongoing presence of discrimination and hostility.

These capitals, or assets, create cultural wealth through the lens of critical race theory.

Both the funds of knowledge framework and community cultural wealth framework challenge the deficit thinking model that many educators and educational leaders have about students of color.

The *funds of knowledge* and *cultural capital* frameworks are important concepts for any educator or educational leader who seeks to understand and connect with students of diverse languages and cultures. Without the acknowledgement and use of these two concepts, English language learners, students in poverty, and other marginalized student groups will continue to be underacknowledged and undervalued, leading to continued achievement gaps for underserved and marginalized students.

Why Do Funds of Knowledge and Cultural Capital Matter?

We are going through one of the most difficult periods in our lives. The COVID-19 pandemic, coupled with a political rhetoric that has targeted immigrants, English language learners, and people of color, have negatively impacted our most vulnerable students and communities. English language learners, students of color, and marginalized students are in our classrooms and they deserve to be educated. These statistics provide additional insight into the *why* we should all feel a sense of urgency:

- Latinx continue to lag other groups when it comes to earning a Bachelors degree. In 2012, 14.5% of Latinx ages 25 and older had a degree. By contrast, 51% of Asians, 34.5% of Whites and 21.2% of Blacks had a Bachelors degree (Lopez & Fry, 2013).
- Spanish was the most common home language for English language learners in 45 states (Lopez & Fry, 2013).
- Overall, English language learner enrollment in public K–12 schools increased by more than one million students, rising from 8.1% of total enrollment to 9.6% (Mitchell, 2020).

We are at the crossroads of change for equity in education. Creating equitable learning communities, establishing high levels of learning for all students, closing opportunity gaps, and eliminating achievement gaps require that we engage in some serious self-reflection and mirror checks. Along with tapping into the funds of knowledge of our students and embracing their cultural capital, we have to face our own implicit biases and beliefs about the students we're working with. The first step can begin with a *mirror check.*

Implicit Bias, Equity, and Mirror Checks

Although the work of creating change that recognizes funds of knowledge and counters implicit bias may feel overwhelming, it can be achieved when change begins within. Countering implicit biases and injustice begins with regular *mirror checks* as we develop awareness about our *own* biased beliefs and behaviors. Those biases and beliefs must be addressed if you're serious about equity and building relationships with students. It is difficult to do the inside-out work, but we can't ignore the impact of our biases on access and academic achievement for students of color.

Implicit bias is defined by the Kirwan Institute for the Study of Race and Ethnicity at the Ohio State University as the "attitudes or stereotypes that affect our understandings, actions, and decisions" (Olinger, 2017) about a certain group of people. The biases can be positive or negative and are usually unconscious and unintentional. Implicit biases, subconscious associations about people, are learned as part of our lived experiences and social conditioning. Most people are unaware that they hold or express implicit bias.

Explicit bias is defined as the attitudes, beliefs and behaviors that one has at the *conscious* level. Examples of explicit bias include negative stereotypes about groups of people, racist rhetoric, hateful speech and discrimination based on race, identity, language, or color. Explicit bias is not only conscious, but intentional and controllable. Explicit bias is hateful and every attempt should be made to keep explicitly biased individuals away from staff and children. We should not accept or tolerate it, especially today when some continue to normalize this type of negative and deliberate hurtful rhetoric.

Mirror checks are a great way to begin to analyze our biases, beliefs, and behaviors. A mirror check helps us understand our authentic selves and our biases. Take a moment to conduct a *mirror check* and ask yourself a few questions:

◆ Do you value diversity?
◆ What are your assumptions about your school community?
◆ Do your students see themselves in your classroom library? In your school?
◆ Are you analyzing data and looking for achievement and opportunity gaps?
◆ Are you taking the time to make connections with every student in your class?
◆ Who are the students that you feel most comfortable connecting with?
◆ Do you view language and culture as an asset or a hindrance to learning?

You may be surprised at your responses to these questions. If you find that you hold biased beliefs about Latinx students, English language learners and/or other groups of historically underserved students, you are not alone and you *can* change things. It is important to keep in mind that we all have implicit biases and that our biases have a tremendous effect on access and achievement in schools. Biases are barriers to learning for many of our students, but especially for students of color and disenfranchised youth. It is important to understand that although we all have biases, we also have the power to change them through reflection and mirror checks. And knowing better means doing better.

Embracing Funds of Knowledge and Cultural Capital

Embracing our student's funds of knowledge and cultural capital require that we resist a historical oppressive system of education. Research and experience indicate that English language learners and students of color are part of a group that has been marginalized and economically disenfranchised. Dolores Delgado-Bernal, a researcher and author, shares that, "for too long, the histories, experiences, cultures, and languages of students of color have been devalued, misinterpreted, or omitted within the formal educational setting" Delgado-Bernal (2002). English language learners have dealt and continue to deal with issues of race, culture, and language in our schools. Those issues negatively affect the overall learning experiences of English language learners and many other students of color.

Paulo Freire's ideas about the banking concept of education as an instrument of oppression (Freire, 2010) deeply resonated with me, especially as they relate to the *funds of knowledge* work. This concept critiques the student–teacher relationship as *narrative*, with the teacher feeding the students facts and "sonority of words" that lack the power to educate or transform. When this occurs, education becomes a banking system "…in which students are the depositories and the teacher is the depositor". Freire concludes that knowledge is more than a mechanical transferring of facts and information. Knowledge is a process of inquiry in which the teacher and student communicate and share knowledge in the world, with the world, and with each other.

This banking system mirrors the oppressive systems that exist in our society. It "serves the interest of the oppressor," (Freire, 2010) maintaining a dominant role while imposing a passive role on the student. It dismisses the student's ability to construct knowledge from the *funds of knowledge* they possess. Students are expected to listen attentively as the teacher teaches, never acknowledging the student as an equal partner in the teaching and learning process who brings with him/her knowledge and cultural capital. The teacher teaches, but whether the student is learning is almost a mystery that can only be solved or proven with standardized testing results, once a year. The student eventually becomes a passive participant in the learning process.

Education is a democratizing process that should be constantly *evolving* and *becoming*. Embracing our students' lived experiences as valuable funds of knowledge and capital experiences is part of a transformative system for many students of color and emerging multilingual students.

How Do I Tap Into My Student's Funds of Knowledge in My Classroom or School?

You've learned about funds of knowledge, cultural capital, implicit bias, explicit bias, and mirror checks. How might we begin to understand our school community's funds of knowledge? How might we begin to tap into the cultural capital that Latinx students and other students of color bring to school to create a richer learning experience? Here are some first-step recommendations:

- Acknowledge your student's lived experiences.
  - This validates a student and assists with the development of relationships.
- Incorporate students' cultural capital, language, and funds of knowledge into your instruction.
  - It is powerful to be able to see yourself reflected in the literature and lessons taught in the classroom.

♦ Build relationships and trust with students and their families.
  ♦ This is easier said than done. Building authentic relationships and trust with your students and families takes time. When families and students understand that you truly care about them, they will go out of their way to learn with and from you.
♦ Develop student voice.
  ♦ Give students opportunities to share in the classroom. Incorporate those opportunities into your lessons across the content areas.
♦ Provide culturally relevant and rigorous learning experiences.
  ♦ Lowering expectations and rigor for English language learners or marginalized students while you connect with kids is not supporting their growth. It is possible to teach at high levels *while* developing relationships with your students.
♦ Interview your students/students' families and attend public events in your student's communities.
  ♦ This is a big part of learning more about your school community, community capital, values, and dreams.
♦ Invite guest speakers from various communities to share traditions, celebrations, or slices of daily life.
♦ Engage parents in learnings, school activities, and celebrations as a way to build connections and understand the community's values, concerns, experiences and dreams:
  ♦ *Family nights*: Showcase the community's funds of knowledge and expertise.
  ♦ *Coffee with the principal*: Meetings where parents can freely and comfortably ask questions of administrators.
  ♦ *Parent academies*: Math, reading, ESL, mental health support throughout the academic year taking place in both the morning and after school.
  ♦ *Volunteers*: Invite parents to come in and support beyond the copy machine. Some parents might feel

that they don't have a lot to share, but ensure that you are tapping into their *funds of knowledge*.

◆ *Storytelling*: Storytelling forges connections between people. Stories highlight the culture, history, and values that unite people in your school community. They highlight the community capital and *funds of knowledge*.

These recommendations are just a few to begin the work of growing as educators for equity and cultural competency. It is impossible to do this work without tapping into our student's cultural capital and resisting oppressive systems of education for English language learners and other marginalized student groups.

Leaders, What Are You Prepared to Do?

We are fortunate to be able to work with students who bring diverse cultural and linguistic funds of knowledge and cultural capital to the schoolhouse. Those experiences and knowledge have been historically perceived as deficits that require "fixing." We've learned that this is not the case and that those strengths and funds of knowledge contribute greatly to learning for every person in our classrooms. In fact, every student reaps the benefits of diversity in our schools.

As leaders, it is our responsibility to model and lead by example in the work of equity and tolerance. This is especially urgent today as our educational practices and systems are founded in a mainstream monolingual and middle class set of educational beliefs and perspectives. I ask you, what are you prepared to do:

◆ In your school?
◆ For your community?
◆ As a leader?

…to tap into the *funds of knowledge* and *cultural capital* of Latinx English language learners, and historically marginalized students?

Conclusion

Our students come to us with a variety of lived experiences, family traditions, funds of knowledge, and cultural capital that we have chosen to cast aside for many years. We worked very hard to quickly modify or eliminate language, culture, while assimilating students into our way of knowing and doing. We had the best of intentions and did not realize the harmful impacts on our students. I know this firsthand, as I have personally experienced it.

I began this chapter by asking you a few important questions:

- ◆ Do you believe that students and their families have something to contribute to learning before they ever enter our classrooms?
- ◆ Do you believe that *students of color* and families with diverse languages and cultures have something to contribute to learning before they ever enter our classrooms?
- ◆ Do you believe that home language, culture, and life experiences are relevant even when they differ from yours?

If we dig deep and answer honestly, our responses to the questions probably include a few nos. Our biases, assumptions, and beliefs about the language and culture of our students greatly influence our behaviors and learning expectations in our classrooms. The diverse cultural and linguistic experiences and knowledge that many of our students bring to the schoolhouse are indeed strengths and funds of knowledge that contribute greatly to learning. This cultural capital and funds of knowledge possessed by students play a vital role in their academic identity, learning and long-term success. We are at the crossroads of change for equity in education and we can begin that change by embracing diversity and tapping into the gifts of culture, race, and language.

Resources

Bennett, C. (2020, August 27). ELL Students' Background Knowledge as an Academic Fund. *ThoughtCo*. Retrieved from www.thoughtco.com/ell-students-funds-of-knowledge-4011987.

Cummins, J., Bismilla, V., Chow, P., Cohen, S., Giampapa, F., Leoni, L., Sandhu, P. and Sastri, P. (2005). Affirming Identity in Multilingual Classrooms. *Educational Leadership*, *63*(1), 38–43.

Delgado-Bernal, D.D. (2002). Critical Race Theory, Latino Critical Theory, and Critical Raced-gendered Epistemologies: Recognizing Students of Color as Holders and Creators of Knowledge. *Qualitative Inquiry*, *8*(1), 105–26.

Freire, P. (2010). *Pedagogy of the Oppressed*. New York: Continuum.

González, N., Moll, L.C. and Amanti, C. (Eds.). (2005). *Funds of Knowledge: Theorizing Practices in Households, Communities, and Classrooms*. New York, NY: Routledge.

Hattie, J. (2009). Visible Learning: A Synthesis of Over 800 Meta-Analyses Relating to Achievement. London: Routledge. https://doi.org/10.4324/9780203887332

Lopez, M. and Fry, R. (2013, September 4). Among Recent High School Grads, Hispanic College Enrollment Rate Surpasses that of Whites. *Pew Research Center*. Retrieved January 28, 2021, from www.pewresearch.org/fact-tank/2013/09/04/hispanic-college-enrollment-rate-surpasses-whites-for-the-first-time.

Mitchell, C. (2020, November 19). The Nation's English-Learner Population Has Surged: 3 Things to Know. *Education Week*. Retrieved January 28, 2021, from www.edweek.org/leadership/the-nations-english-learner-population-has-surged-3-things-to-know/2020/02.

Olinger, J. (2017, August 23). Chipping Away at Implicit Bias. *Kirwan Institute for the Study of Race and Ethnicity*. Retrieved January 28, 2021, from https://kirwaninstitute.osu.edu/article/chipping-away-implicit-bias.

Saathoff, S.D. (2015). Funds of Knowledge and Community Cultural Wealth: Exploring how Pre-Service Teachers can Work Effectively with Mexican and Mexican American Students. *Critical Questions in Education*, *6*(1), 30–40.

Yosso, T.J. (2005). Whose Culture has Capital? A Critical Race Theory Discussion of Community Cultural Wealth. *Race Ethnicity and Education*, *8*(1), 69–91.

3

Equity in Early Childhood Education

Marcie Faust

Historically, early childhood education was a luxury for families who had the means to provide early educational experiences for their children. Today, advocates for early childhood education recommend high quality educational experiences for all children to promote intellectual, language, physical, social and emotional development to build a foundation for school readiness. Unfortunately, for many families, a number of barriers exist that prevent all children from participating in an early childhood program that supports their development and ensures school readiness. Some barriers include the limited availability of programs in certain communities, a need for additional childcare hours for working families, and the financial burden of high tuition prices. Because a child's education is not publicly subsidized until the age of five, families face difficult decisions about their child's early education experience before they reach kindergarten.

Embracing inclusivity and diversity among young students is the professional obligation of all early childhood professionals. This chapter explores ways to advance equity in early childhood education, address biases, reflect on current practices, and design programs and opportunities to help *all* young children reach their full potential.

Equity for At-Risk Groups of Early Childhood Students

In many communities, early childhood education is not a question of *if*, it's a question of *when*. Depending on the childcare needs of the family, many parents seek early childhood options when their child is still an infant. Before children reach the age of three, many parents rely on early childhood educational opportunities to meet their childcare needs. As children reach the age of three or four years old, parents frequently seek out an early childhood program to teach school readiness skills to their child. Equity for young children is imperative to give them every advantage to succeed when they enter into kindergarten and beyond. The following section breaks down at-risk groups of children and discusses ways to provide them with an equitable and impactful early childhood education experience. Suggestions to improve equity among at-risk groups of children will also be discussed.

Early Childhood Students from Low-Income Families

The federally-funded Head Start and Early Head Start programs exist to promote school readiness of children ages birth to five from low-income families by supporting the development of the whole child (Office of Head Start, 2019). For young children under the age of three, early childhood programs for low-income families are served through licensed day care centers, family childcare homes, or federally-funded Early Head Start classrooms. Even with the availability of these programs, parents may not be able to access them due to their location, language barriers, immigration concerns, and cultural preferences. Providing equity to low-income families becomes an increasing challenge if parents cannot access early childhood programs.

As children become older, however, and reach the age of three and four years old, more programs become available to families without tuition fees. For example, public and charter schools frequently provide pre-K programs for children between the ages of three to five, utilizing grants and federal funds to cover the cost of tuition. As more opportunities for early childhood education arise through community-based programs, a frequent downside involves a lack of diversity or socioeconomic integration.

The composition of the early childhood classroom plays an important role in providing equitable learning conditions for low-income students. Socioeconomic diversity among early childhood students extends opportunities for them to interact with and learn from one another. Because higher skill levels among children are frequently associated with higher average socioeconomic status (SES), children of higher than average SES can positively impact the skills of their lower than average SES peers. For example, children with stronger expressive and receptive language skills developed at home can influence those skills among their peers. Programs that attract children of diverse backgrounds have a better chance of supporting the development of low-income children.

Other ways of ensuring equity among low-income children in early childhood programs include free or affordable programs, parent outreach campaigns, and attracting highly trained teachers. Program leaders and coordinators can work with organizations and connection channels such as public libraries and community centers to notify and attract diverse families to their school's program.

Early Childhood Students with Special Needs

As mentioned earlier, children learn by interacting with their peers. Just as low-income students who come to school with less developed skills can learn from their peers, the same philosophy exists for early childhood students with special needs. Peer models serve as powerful examples for students with special needs to follow. Learning to interact through play, building language skills, as well as social-emotional skills can all be learning experiences when a child with special needs observes, mirrors, and engages with a developing peer who does not have such needs. For this reason, the inclusion of children with special needs in early childhood classrooms is imperative to enhance access, participation, and learning outcomes for all early childhood students.

In early childhood classrooms, inclusion is the pathway toward equity. Being careful not to confuse equity with equality, early childhood educators must recognize that not all students should be given the same opportunities. Accommodations and modifications for children with special needs make it possible for these young children to thrive. An example of providing an equitable opportunity might be a child who uses an iPad for augmentative and alternative communication. Not all children benefit from access to an iPad, but the device opens language opportunities for children with special needs to help them access their educational environment and participate in learning experiences in a similar way to their peers. This example demonstrates how an inclusionary practice of providing a child with an assistive device for communication provides the child with an equitable learning opportunity.

Early childhood classrooms that include children with special needs make it possible for children with disabilities to learn and thrive, while teaching children without such needs to develop respect, tolerance of differences, and acceptance of others. Teachers who are committed to inclusion and equity recognize the effectiveness of blending children of varying abilities and skills into the same classroom community of learners.

Early Childhood Students Learning English

As schools and communities become more diverse in terms of cultural and linguistic diversity, early childhood educators must be prepared for teaching and learning in cross-racial, cross-ethnic, and cross-cultural situations (Lee, Butler, & Tippins, 2007; Vittrup, 2016). English language learners (ELLs) account for an increasing number of children in our schools, and finding ways to ensure that ELL's have access to educational programs that support their learning of the English language is essential. For this group of young students, an equitable learning environment involves individualizing the teacher's instructional methods, contents, and materials to address in a sensitive way the variation in children's cultural and linguistic backgrounds.

To support young children learning English, ELL's in early childhood classrooms are encouraged to continue using their heritage language to help them maintain their heritage language skills while finding connections between both languages. Teachers can also provide young ELLs with written and visual materials to help them access their educational environment and develop their literacy skills. In addition, giving young ELLs opportunities to speak with their English-speaking peers is an authentic way to help children develop literacy skills through social interaction.

Once again, the power of diversity among children in early childhood classrooms paves the way for equity for all learners. When diversity and inclusion are valued, equitable experiences for ELLs in early childhood settings become the norm.

Addressing Biases in Early Childhood Classrooms

As described in the previous section, children in at-risk populations (low-income students, students with special needs, ELLs) contribute to the diversity within our early childhood classrooms. In addition, as our society continues to become increasingly diverse, our classrooms represent a range of backgrounds among our students. As young children enter early childhood classrooms, educators have a responsibility to provide students with tools that they need to understand differences, stand up for injustice, and reflect on their own thoughts and actions. The following section examines three ways in which educators and school leaders can avoid bias in the classroom to ensure that young children are provided with equitable access to their education.

Recognizing Microaggressions

Microaggressions, according to Sue et al. (2007) are "brief and commonplace daily verbal, behavioral, or environmental indignities, whether intentional or unintentional, that communicate hostile, derogatory, or negative racial slights and insults toward people of color." Examples of microaggressions that early childhood teachers may unintentionally exhibit include some of the following:

- ◆ Failing to learn to pronounce or continuing to mispronounce the names of students after being corrected by the student.
- ◆ Setting low expectations for particular groups of students.
- ◆ Singling students out in a group discussion solely because of their background.
- ◆ Reading picture books that only represent White characters rather than characters of diverse backgrounds.

Early childhood educators may not notice these microaggressions, but acknowledging and addressing them will help students feel accepted and safe. Similarly, it is important for educators to notice and put a stop to microaggressions as they happen in classrooms. For example, if a child makes a comment about the appearance of another child's hair or skin, educators should acknowledge these statements. Picture books can help early childhood educators address these issues in their classrooms to engage young children in conversations about microaggressions. The following titles either address microaggressions explicitly or tell the story of a child on the receiving end of them (Turner, 2019):

- ◆ *Ouch! Moments: When Words Are Used in Hurtful Ways*, written by Michael Genhart, illustrated by Viviana Garofoli.
- ◆ *I Am René, the Boy/Soy René, el Niño*, written by René Colato Laínez, illustrated by Fabiolla Graullera Ramírez.
- ◆ *Don't Touch My Hair*, written and illustrated by Sharee Miller.
- ◆ *10,000 Dresses* by Marcus Ewert, illustrated by Rex Ray.
- ◆ *The Name Jar*, written and illustrated by Yangsook Choi.

The negative messages that are received by early childhood students can be particularly damaging during the formative years of a young child's development. Children need to feel emotionally safe in their learning environment in order to learn and thrive. Educators must affirm positive attributes about all children in a classroom and intervene when they witness microaggressions between students. In addition, educators have a responsibility to examine their own biases and microaggressive language to ensure a safe, supportive, inclusive classroom community for all young children.

Auditing Learning Materials

As the previous section points out, picture books can serve as a powerful tool to help teach students about microaggressive language. Frequently auditing classroom materials to ensure that students have access to racially, ethnically, and culturally diverse materials will lead to more equitable classroom environments. Examples of diverse learning materials in an early childhood classroom include:

- ◆ Present dolls representing a variety of races.
- ◆ Showcase food that represents a variety of cultures and ethnicities.
- ◆ Explore music that represents cultural and ethnic diversity.
- ◆ Display and highlight picture books and posters with characters or images that represent differences across race, gender, and sexual identity.

For teachers to engage in equitable and inclusive teaching practices, critically reading and rereading curriculum and teaching materials also includes naming and addressing inequities enacted by the materials (Souto-Manning et al., 2019). When children do not see themselves represented in their classroom, it gives them the impression that they do not belong. In contrast, an overrepresentation of some groups of students in classroom materials can lead to an inflated impression that one group is superior to another. When teachers take the time to audit their classroom materials, they advance equity and inclusion in their classroom by taking action in making them more representative and inclusive.

Maintaining High Expectations

Teacher expectations are a strong predictor of student outcomes, yet teachers frequently lower expectations for their students. This implicit bias may affect students of a minority race or ethnicity and/or a young child with a disability. Examples may include a teacher viewing a child of an ethnic minority as "being less intelligent" or a child with a disability as "never capable of learning a particular skill." While the expected outcomes for ELLs or children with disabilities may need to be adjusted based on their current skill level, lowering expectations can lead to a self-fulfilling prophecy where predictors of an expected outcome cause that outcome to actually occur. Early childhood educators are therefore encouraged to communicate high expectations to all students, as well as their families, as they influence young children's motivation, self-esteem, and self-concept.

Early childhood educators who have high expectations tend to take greater responsibility for their students' learning (Halvorsen, Lee & Andrade, 2009). Educators with a strong sense of responsibility will examine their own teaching practices when students are not responding and make changes to improve outcomes for that child (Guo et al., 2010). This can lead to additional time spent on designing individualized supports for students, as well as collaborating with other staff members who may provide a new perspective or approach to help the young learner. Teachers who recognize the value of high expectations for *every* child affirm the diverse cultures, learning styles, and abilities of their students, while taking responsibility for their learning and development.

Current Practices that Encourage Equity

To achieve equity in an early childhood classroom, teachers must reflect critically on their current practices. The previous section provided examples of how to address the biases of early childhood educators, which opens the door for reflection about how current practices can be intentionally developed to support the educational needs of young children. The following section provides examples of best practices for early childhood classrooms in which equity and inclusion are promoted, and intended outcomes for all children are individualized.

Differentiation

A differentiated learning environment for early childhood students allows educators to respond to children's unique strengths, abilities, learning styles, and interests. From an equity lens, this approach gives each child a range of learning experiences at their readiness level so that all children have access to opportunities and resources. Tomlinson & Moon (2014) identified four classroom elements that educators can adjust for all students: (1) content—what the students need to learn or how the student will access the information, (2) process—activities in which students engage in order to make sense or master the content, (3) products—projects that ask students to rehearse, apply, and extend what they have learned, and (4) learning environment—the way the classroom works and feels.

In an early childhood classroom, content can be a unit of study about a topic that can appear very basic but expand to include complex ideas. An example may be a unit on trees, which begins with an investigation about the parts of a tree but expands to include experiences that allow students to interact with actual parts of trees by classifying and sorting tree parts, photographing and compiling tree photographs, and writing a class story about why trees are important and need protection. As the young children engage in the content, opportunities for differentiation help the teacher build on students' current skills and interests so that all students have the opportunity to find meaning in the learning experience.

Differentiated processes in early childhood classrooms include a range of activities that provide active learning for all children. These activities can include interest-based centers or whole class tasks. Using the tree unit example, differentiated processes could include a dramatic play area where children go to an apple orchard to pick and sell apples, or a counting and sorting area where children examine the different colors of apples or the numbers of seeds. Using differentiation, the length of time a child engages in the activities, the complexity of the task, and the amount of adult facilitation can be varied so that all students can participate in common learning experiences that are meaningful to them.

Another form of differentiation that teachers can provide to students in early childhood classrooms includes the products that students need to produce. Students can work together or alone on parts of a large mural where some emergent writers label pictures while others add colors or details. Another way to differentiate products may be through an interactive read aloud where students are given different roles in the reading of a shared book with some students reciting lines from the story while others act out different parts. Additionally, the use of drawing, writing, singing, and storytelling for early childhood students allows them to engage with various product options that are appropriate and accessible to their levels of learning.

The last form of differentiation includes the learning environment, which plays a critical role in student learning among early childhood classrooms. Classrooms for young children should be inviting and organized, with clearly marked designated areas for various learning activities. For example:

- ◆ An open rug with designated supportive seating options for students who need them, makes it possible for all children to sit together in a whole group setting and learn alongside one another.
- ◆ Choice areas can be clearly marked with words and pictures to provide visual support to students so that they know where to go in the classroom.
- ◆ Established routines for students so that they can independently make choices and ask for help when they need it.

In addition, the materials displayed in the classroom need to represent intercultural attributes so that the learning space reflects children's different backgrounds, cultures, family structures, and abilities. By creating a supportive environment that is conducive to differentiation, all students have equitable access to experiences that help them learn and grow.

Inclusive Practices

Young children with disabilities should have access to inclusive high quality early childhood programs, where they are provided with individualized and appropriate support in meeting high expectations (US Department of Health and Human Services & US Department of Education, 2015). Under this provision, early childhood students should receive special education services in learning environments that allow children with disabilities to socialize and play with children who are typically developing. In order to make this learning experience possible for children with disabilities, early childhood special education teachers and related services providers must integrate services into blended classrooms. Through a blended model, educators and therapists can collaborate with each other, along with the student's family to identify the best options for inclusive services in community-based settings (Sandall & Schwartz, 2002).

Inclusive practices in early childhood classrooms are the gateway to ensuring equity of access to high quality education for all children. Early childhood educators who are committed to developing inclusive environments understand that children with disabilities are entitled to equal opportunities to fully participate in all experiences, activities, and events alongside their same-age peers. When preschool-age children with disabilities have complete access to the same opportunities as their developing peers who do not have a disability, as well as the support and accommodations necessary to learn and grow, it sends an important message that all young children are entitled to an education that is individually appropriate.

Suggestions for Program Supports

To help young children reach their full potential during the years leading up to kindergarten, early childhood programs can be strengthened by scaffolding support around the students and teachers. The following section provides suggestions that can improve equitable access for all young children in early childhood programs.

Parental Engagement

Early childhood educators are encouraged to partner with families to support the learning and development of preschool-age children at home. One of the greatest challenges for parents of this young age group is that they either did not attend an early childhood program when they were a young child or they attended prior to their memory. While parents have memories of being an elementary-age student, parents are less likely to intuitively understand how to support early childhood experiences for their children because they don't have those experiences in their collective memory. Without memories of this period of their life or a background in child development, it is understandable that many parents may not have the skills to support and advocate for their child's learning. Opportunities for parent involvement and education can help provide parents with strategies and tools to help them become meaningfully engaged in their child's learning.

The National Association for the Education of Young Children (NAEYC) published five recommendations for ways educators can establish reciprocal relationships with families to advance equity among students (NAEYC, n.d.):

1. Embrace the primary role of families in children's development and learning.
2. Uphold every family's right to make decisions for and with their children.
3. Be curious, making time to learn about the families with whom you work.
4. Maintain consistently high expectations for family involvement, being open to multiple and varied forms of engagement and providing intentional and responsive supports.
5. Communicate the values of multilingualism to all families.

Early childhood programs and educators are encouraged to come together to engage and involve families in the child's learning. Like children, parents need different levels of support, and by recognizing the value of parental involvement, engagement, and education, early childhood educators can advance equity for all of their students.

Professional Development for Early Childhood Educators

To strengthen any early childhood program, the professional development of practicing early childhood educators is vitally important to the quality of experiences afforded to children (Martinez-Beck & Zaslow, 2006). A variety of professional development structures can be effective for early childhood educators, but coaching, training, and communities of practice are some of the methods that have been found to effectively promote the growth and development of this particular group of practitioners (Sheridan et al., 2009).

> **Coaching:** An effective professional development vehicle for early childhood educators is coaching. The coach can observe the early childhood educator in practice while collecting data on the interactions between teachers and students, teachers and support staff, and student-to-student interactions. Using this model, the coach is able to identify opportunities for improvement in the areas of inclusion, differentiation, behavior, curriculum, and classroom organization and management. High quality teachers can be developed in the early childhood classrooms, and investing in this model of professional development can lead to well trained and well supported professionals who are more likely to return to the classroom year after year.

> **Training:** In early childhood programs, training can include activities and workshops that provide specific skills for on-the-job application. This format of training can provide general knowledge to a group of early childhood practitioners, but it frequently lacks the follow-up with or feedback to the educators (Pianta, 2006). Though this type of professional development may not be as in-depth or individualized as coaching, it still has a place to improve aspects of early childhood programs. Examples of specialized training that could be useful include sessions on play-based learning,

early childhood milestones, calm down strategies, or fine motor activities. These types of training sessions are helpful to provide educators with opportunities to engage in relevant topics, yet they may not provide the educator with the level of depth that can come from coaching.

Communities of practice: While coaching and training are essential to provide early childhood educators with professional development that suits their background, needs, and interests, learning communities among practitioners also plays a critical role. The term *community of practice* was first introduced by Lave and Wenger (1991) as a way to describe the situated learning that takes place in apprenticeship, a model of learning that involves a complex set of social relationships by which experts pass on knowledge to novices. In communities of practice, early childhood educators can learn alongside one another to review students' work and share recorded or documented classroom observations. These groups provide opportunities for educators to focus on issues, problems, or successes that they encounter in their early childhood classrooms which are highly applicable for all participants because the examples emerge from their own experiences (Sheridan et al., 2009).

Conclusion

Providing young children with equitable learning opportunities makes it possible for all children to reach their full potential. High quality early childhood programs that focus on inclusion and diversity, celebrating the uniqueness of all children, will pave the way for every child to learn, grow, and develop as a valued member of society. By becoming aware of implicit biases, educators can alter how they speak to young children and establish learning environments that are representative and welcoming to everyone. In addition to recognizing biases, early childhood educators are also invited to consider their current practices that promote equity, inclusion, and intended outcomes for all children. Finally, through parent engagement and professional development, educators of young children can strengthen the support provided to children to encourage equity for all. As early childhood educators come together to advance equity, embrace diversity, and promote full inclusion, children will have greater opportunities for lifelong success and learning.

Resources

García, O., Kleifgen, J.A. and Falchi, L. (2008). From English Language Learners to Emergent Bilinguals. Equity Matters. Research Review No. 1. *Campaign for Educational Equity, Teachers College, Columbia University*.

Guo, Y., Piasta, S.B., Justice, L.M. and Kaderavek, J.N. (2010). Relations Among Preschool Teachers' Self-efficacy, Classroom Quality, and Children's Language and Literacy Gains. *Teaching and Teacher Education*, *26*(4), 1094–103.

Halvorsen, A.L., Lee, V.E. and Andrade, F.H. (2009). A Mixed-method Study of Teachers' Attitudes about Teaching in Urban and Low-income Schools. Urban Education, *44*(2), 181–224.

Lave, J. and Wenger, E. (1991). *Situated Learning: Legitimate Peripheral Participation*. Cambridge, UK: Cambridge University Press.

Lee, S., Butler, M.B. and Tippins, D.J. (2007). A Case Study of an Early Childhood Teacher's Perspective on Working with English Language Learners. *Multicultural Education*, *15*(1), 43–9.

Martinez-Beck, I. and Zaslow, M. (2006). Introduction: The Context for Critical Issues in Early Childhood Professional Development. In M. Zaslow and I. Martinez-Beck (Eds.), *Critical Issues in Early Childhood Professional Development* (p. 1–6). Baltimore: Paul H. Brookes.

NAEYC. (n.d.). *Recommendations for Early Childhood Educators*. Retrieved August 30, 2020, from www.naeyc.org/resources/position-statements/equity/recommendations-ECE.

Office of Head Start. (2019, February 11). Head Start Services. www.acf.hhs.gov/ohs/about/head-start.

Pianta, R.C. (2006). Standardized Observation and Professional Development: A focus on individualized implementation and practices. In M. Zaslow and I. Martinez-Beck (Eds.), *Critical Issues in Early Childhood Professional Development* (pp. 231–54). Baltimore: Paul H. Brookes.

Reid, J.L. (2012). Socioeconomic Diversity and Early Learning: The Missing Link in Policy for High-Quality Preschools. In R. Kahlenberg. (Ed.), The Future of School Integration: Socioeconomic Diversity as an Education Reform Strategy. New York, NY: The Century Foundation.

Reid, J.L. and Kagan, S.L. (2015). *A Better Start: Why Classroom Diversity Matters in Early Education*. The Century Foundation and Poverty & Race Research Action Council.

Sandall, S. and Schwartz, I. (2002). *Building Blocks for Teaching Preschoolers with Special Needs*. Baltimore: Paul H. Brookes.

Sheridan, S.M., Edwards, C.P., Marvin, C.A. and Knoche, L.L. (2009). Professional Development in Early Childhood Programs: Process Issues and Research Needs. *Early Education and Development*, *20*(3), 377–401.

Souto-Manning, M., Rabadi-Raol, A., Robinson, D. and Perez, A. (2019). What Stories do my Classroom and its Materials Tell? Preparing Early Childhood Teachers to Engage in Equitable and Inclusive Teaching. *Young Exceptional Children*, *22*(2), 62–73.

Sue, D.W., Capodilupo, C.M., Torino, G.C., Bucceri, J.M., Holder, A.M., Nadal, K.L. and Esquilin, M. (2007). Racial Microaggressions in Everyday Life: Implications for Clinical Practice. *American Psychologist*. *62*(4), 271–86.

Tomlinson, C.A. and Moon, T.R. (2014). *Assessment and Student Success in a Differentiated Classroom*. Cheltenham, VIC: Hawker Brownlow Education.

Turner, B. (2019, March 26). Teaching First-Graders About Micro-aggressions: The Small Moments Add Up. *Teaching Tolerance*. www.tolerance.org/magazine/teaching-firstgraders-about-microaggressions-the-small-moments-add-up.

US Department of Health and Human Services and US Department of Education. (2015). Policy Statement on Inclusion of Children With Disabilities in Early Childhood Programs. *Infants & Young Children*, *29*(1), 3–24.

Vittrup, B. (2016). Early Childhood Teachers' Approaches to Multicultural Education and Perceived Barriers to Disseminating Anti-bias Messages. *Multicultural Education*, *23*(3-4), 37–41.

4

Equity of Access
Moving Beyond the Barriers that Limit Opportunities for All Students

Kim Hofmann

Throughout my almost 20-year career in education, my work has primarily been focused on supporting students in "special populations." Those groups of students that are different are not considered to be part of the general population. Examples include special education, English language learners, students of low socioeconomic status, and the list continues. I am incredibly passionate about not only equalizing opportunities for kids but also ensuring every kid gets the support they need to be successful in life. Being a voice for students who often have limited access to educational opportunities continues to be my passion. Increasing student voice is accomplished by working collaboratively with teachers and leaders to ensure all kids find success within their schools' walls. Yes, that overused phrase "all means all," this phrase is "my jam," as my kids would say. Educators who are committed to doing whatever they can to ensure all kids have the same educational opportunities. Ensuring that regardless of home life, age level, background, ethnicity, socioeconomic status, gender identification, sexual orientation or ability level, all students can, not only access our educational system, but also access any additional support needed to be successful within our educational system. The African proverb, "it takes a village to raise a child", rings true here. We, as educators, are the village. It takes every one of us working together to support students and make sure they have access to their education. No one can do this alone. Not one of us has all of the answers, but together, we can make a difference. We, as educators, have an amazing opportunity and incredible responsibility.

Equity in education ensures access for students from all backgrounds and all performance levels. The core of equity is about getting to know kids, understanding who they are and how to support them. It is important for educators to maintain high expectations for all students but recognize that the path for students to get there may be different and require providing students with the opportunity to access all subjects and courses, which appears to be no easy task (Blankstein & Noguera, 2016). However, schools across the country continue to track students and create obstacles for all students to access grade level and advanced courses. Not only does the delivery of curriculum impact access, but overall educator beliefs do as well. The research demonstrates the benefits and improved outcomes for students exposed to high-level curriculum and high expectations. So, why do schools struggle with ensuring access for all kids? We will explore the barriers schools face and a number of opportunities to break down the barriers inhibiting access for all kids. How do we, as educators, ensure equity of access? How do we not only make this promise to every student but also guarantee that we deliver on our promises?

Achieving equitable access for all kids requires that educators focus on creating pathways for all kids, creating opportunities for all kids. We believe all kids can learn. All means all. These are common phrases in education. Without a doubt, educators believe all kids can learn and they will do whatever it takes to support students to be successful. What does this look like in schools? What behaviors do teachers and leaders engage in that support the belief all kids can learn? How do our beliefs manifest themselves in our schools? Let's begin by looking at what equitable access looks like in a classroom. Creating pathways for students who need them starts with the belief systems of the adults within the schools.

Barrier 1: Beliefs

As educators, beliefs are at the foundation of our work. Our beliefs influence how we approach and support students. Expectations are embedded in our beliefs, making it imperative for us to be aware and in tune with our beliefs. Reflecting on our beliefs is critical. The reflection should include consideration of how our behaviors align with our beliefs. For instance, when a stranger walks into your classroom or school building, how would they know there are high expectations for all kids? What does it look like to have high expectations in the classroom? Do we walk the talk? It comes naturally to say we, as educators, believe all kids can learn. It is an entirely different thing to ensure our actions support our beliefs. Many times systems within our schools inhibit our ability to align our behavior with our beliefs.

To illustrate the importance of beliefs, let's review, in my opinion, a much-underutilized research project. This research project provides vital information regarding the role our expectations play in influencing others' behaviors. In 1968, a Harvard psychologist, Robert Rosenthal, conducted a study within an elementary school in California. Rosenthal and his colleague Jacobson administered intelligence pre-tests and then randomly selected 20% of the students to create a group. The researchers informed teachers that the students were primed to excel in the classroom based on the results of their intelligence pre-test. The teachers did not know the students were randomly selected and that the pre-test results had no impact on why they were chosen. After eight months, the students were tested again. Results showed their performance increased significantly despite the students' intellectual pre-screening results. The study concluded that high teacher expectations lead to higher performance, and lower teacher expectations lead to lower performance.

This phenomenon was termed the "Pygmalion effect", after the mythological Greek sculptor whose love for the ivory statue of a woman he created inspired the gods to bring her to life. There is immense power in high expectations. As educators, we should be striving to harness this power to positively impact students.

Research states clearly our attitudes and beliefs directly impact student performance in the classroom. How can we ensure we are utilizing this to our advantage? For me, it starts with hiring. As part of the hiring process, I engage candidates in a scripted screening process. Through the process, I ask candidates a question regarding high expectations for all students. Is it possible? Believe it or not, several candidates answer no to this question. Although this screening question is one of many, the answer to the question, in particular, is very revealing. It quickly lets you know if the candidate believes you can have high expectations for all kids. If they do, they typically promptly follow up with several comments or examples of why and how this impacts their instruction. Having high expectations for all students is a powerful tool to ensure equity of opportunity and support in order for all students to engage in the curriculum. The hiring process is an excellent opportunity to ensure we hire staff that will maintain high expectations for kids. We must believe all students can learn. In what other ways can we make certain we are taking advantage of this knowledge?

Opportunities

◆ Put your high expectations to work. When teaching difficult material or assigning difficult tasks, tell your students you know it is challenging, but you believe they can do it! As always, if you feel the task is too demanding, take a step back and reteach as needed.

◆ Keep conversations among staff focused on high expectations for students. As a leader, provide support and feedback to staff throughout the year. Doing so will encourage staff to continue to set high expectations for students.

◆ Engage in honest conversations about what is happening with kids. Create a safe space among grade level teachers and staff in the building for critical discussions that will support students and move the conversation forward. Sharing what is working and the challenges you face with students in a collaborative setting is very beneficial for students.

◆ Work to keep the teacher's lounge talk positive. Most certainly, our work as educators can be extremely stressful and frustrating. However, all too often, the teacher's lounge can be a place where negative comments and frustrations abound. It takes maintaining a "can-do" attitude to ensure we remain optimistic in our work and committed to high expectations.

◆ Incorporate questions regarding expectations when hiring teachers, administrators, and support staff. After hiring staff, observe how they demonstrate their high expectations for students. Be sure to acknowledge staff who verbalize high expectations and provide whatever support is necessary for students to succeed.

Barrier 2: Schedules

The school schedule, elementary through secondary, tends to be one of the most significant roadblocks to providing equitable access to all students. As leaders reflect on traditional scheduling practices, challenges can be identified. Identifying challenges provides leaders the opportunity to begin to make adjustments where needed. In order to bring to light how this plays out in schools, it is best to look at a few examples. Indeed, there is no ill intent when developing schedules and providing support services. However, reflecting on our practices with an open mind and spirit of continual improvement creates opportunities for schools to increase access for all kids.

In this first example, we will explore the use of remedial courses. Certainly, these courses and scheduling practices were created with the desire to support students. However, in doing so, educators inadvertently lowered expectations for the students. Likely, in part, due to the No Child Left Behind Act of 2001 and the focus on student outcomes, there is now widespread use of remedial core courses, such as English and math. These courses lower expectations, cover fewer standards, and slow down the delivery of content.

Let's look at a few very typical scenarios that occur in high schools. When scheduling a student into remedial reading, the student is often forced into remedial math class based on the timing of course offerings. If you are a student with special needs and have a reading goal, you are then placed into a remedial math course because that reflects the special education teachers' schedule. Now let's take a student that is an English language learner. Given that the student is an English language learner, the student's placement is a lower level English course instead of the grade level English course. These are just a few of several examples of how our scheduling practices create inequitable access to general education courses.

From an elementary perspective, limited access also takes place. Concepts like "alternate core" actually had traction in some districts. An alternate core alters students' access to the core curriculum. Let's talk through what an alternate core looks like. Students that score below a certain threshold are grouped based on ability level. Reading instruction within an elementary school is typically scheduled for a minimum 90-minute block daily. Students who scored below the threshold are grouped and leave the general education classroom and go to an alternate location for instruction during this reading block. The instruction occurring in the alternate location is not grade level content. The students who remain in the classroom have scored higher on the assessment, so they remain and receive grade level reading content. So, what happens? Students in the alternate core do not have exposure to the general education curriculum, subsequently putting these students further and further behind.

Another example that can occur at any grade level, but is most prominent in elementary and middle schools, is the service delivery of special programs. For instance, if a student has reading services on their individualized education program (IEP), too often, these students are taken out of the reading block while core instruction is taking place. Removing students from the general education classroom to provide intervention supports also happens frequently. Unfortunately, the same students who need intervention support also need access to the general education content. English language learners, students with behavior challenges, and any student who needs something a little more, regardless of what that might be, also experience being removed from the general education classroom to receive necessary support.

There is tremendous value in exposing all kids, regardless of circumstances, to the general education curriculum. Engagement in the general education classroom is essential. Schools should strive to provide differentiation and support within the general education setting to deter the schedule from driving student decisions. When working on schedules or any decision-making with students, remain student-centered, and schedule or access to courses will no longer be a barrier.

Opportunities

♦ Remove requirements that limit a student's access to higher level courses. Why would we discourage students that tell us they want to take more challenging classes? If a student wants to challenge themselves and take a course that we, as the adults, do not feel the student should take, talk to the student. Share expectations of the class. Provide the student a chance to share their voice and agency before telling them the course is not an option. Support students that want to challenge themselves. Instead of telling them they do not have access to more rigorous courses, ask what support they might need while taking the class.

♦ Eliminate tracking. Stop allowing test scores from middle school to determine access to rigorous courses in high school. It is all too common that students take exams in middle school that then place them in the honors level track. An assessment from middle school becomes students' only opportunity to access an honors level or more rigorous courses. For example, in most schools, students need to take algebra as an 8eighth-grade student to have the opportunity to take the highest level of math in high school. The invitation to take algebra as an eighth grader is a result of test scores. Many schools have a practice to utilize standardized test scores from the fifth or sixth grade to determine the track students will be placed in for seventh and eighth grade, therefore locking a student in a predetermined track in high school. I experienced this with my daughter. She did not qualify to take algebra as an eighth grader; therefore, the only way for her to take the highest level of math offered in high school was to double up math courses while in high school. As a freshman, when asked if she could double up math courses, she was told "no, we don't allow that." How does it make sense we would refuse to let a student advance in math due to a test she took in the sixth grade?

◆ Analyze students taking AP courses, honors courses, and college prep courses. Who is taking them? Is it representative of your student population? This data is very enlightening. Many times the students taking higher level courses do not reflect the student population. The same is true in the reverse. Also look at which students are scheduled into lower level courses. It is very likely this data is also not reflective of your student population. Of course, looking at data is excellent, but we know that is only the first step. What story does it tell? Are we happy with the story it is telling about our school?

◆ Remove remedial courses from the schedule or make adjustments to how these courses are utilized. Many schools across the country have developed remedial math and English courses for students who have been determined would not be successful in the general education environment. These courses are typically a watered down version of the curriculum and often taught at a much slower pace. Although we know there were good intentions when developing these types of courses, they are very harmful to kids. Research is clear that children are more successful if they have access to the general education classroom (Gamoran et al., 1995; Shearer, 1967).

The benefits of access to the general education curriculum apply to all students, whether they have a disability, a history of low performance in school or any other circumstance that comes to mind.

♦ Develop student-centered schedules. A schedule that supports the student as opposed to a schedule that serves department, grade level or building needs. Beginning with student needs in mind, schools develop a protocol gathering multiple data points such as grades, attendance, discipline, engagement, strengths and needs of students and most importantly, student voice. The school then utilizes this data to develop the master schedule. I have engaged in this process and observed the benefits for all students, including those students identified in the "special populations" (special needs, at-risk, English language learners, low socioeconomic status).

♦ Do students have the opportunity for additional support without missing core instruction? If a student needs extra support in reading, do they have to miss reading class to get it?

Barrier 3: Systems

All students need some level of support to navigate school successfully. The support can come in many different forms, including academic, extra time, social-emotional. Most schools have some type of mechanism in place; however, some systems are not as effective as they could be. In order to have equal opportunities for students and support for students to engage in those opportunities, schools need to implement research-based frameworks that are student-centered and responsive to student needs.

Two key concepts, multitiered system of supports (MTSS) and culturally responsive teaching (CRT), are proven frameworks that increase instructional engagement for all kids, including students from diverse backgrounds. Both frameworks are proven to increase outcomes for all students (Larson et al., 2018; Howard & Terry Sr., 2011; Vermeer, 2017).

CRT isn't a program or a thing. It is a way of teaching that is intentional and visible in all aspects of instruction. In my experience, CRT is about being respectful and understanding of the various cultures within your classroom and, in doing so, creates several advantages for students that increase their overall performance within the classroom. The CRT framework supports higher expectations by focusing on students' strengths rather than student deficits. A bona fide CRT classroom empowers students in their learning by increasing student voice and choice in their learning. The inclusive nature of CRT builds an understanding of varying perspectives and helps all students in the classroom recognize one another's strengths (Griner & Stewart, 2013).

MTSS guarantees students will receive the support they need when they need it. Students have access to a variety of supports that vary in intensity. Formative assessment data provides guidance to teachers to connect students with the appropriate support. One of the key elements for MTSS is that it is systematic. All kids, regardless of need, classroom, circumstances, receive what they need.

Both frameworks, CRT and MTSS, begin with the leader. Building leaders have an opportunity and responsibility to support the infusion of both frameworks to ensure all students have every opportunity to learn from their teachers, classmates, and the entire school community. In *Uniting Academic and Behavior Interventions: Solving the Skill Or Will Dilemma* (Buffum et al., 2015), four critical principles are outlined. The four principles are the cultural foundation within schools, also known as the four Cs. The four Cs comprise the following: collective responsibility, concentrated instruction, convergent assessment, and certain access. Below is a brief description of each.

Collective responsibility: The idea that all adults are responsible for all kids within the school. With that, all adults will do whatever it takes to help students be successful.

Concentrated instruction: The idea that every grade level and every teacher is crystal clear on expected outcomes for the year.

Convergent assessment: Teachers collect common data around instructional concepts. Data is collected across classrooms and content areas and is analyzed by teacher teams to connect kids with the appropriate support.

Certain access: All students are guaranteed additional time and support to master grade level content.

All four of these principles are essential in building a collaborative culture that is hyper-focused on student success. A potent activity is to engage staff in conversations around these four concepts. Where would they rate their classroom, department, or school building around each of the four Cs? Although all four concepts are essential to building a culture that supports students, certain access, in my opinion, is the most critical concept.

Mike Mattos, the guru of MTSS, often speaks about the promise we should all be making to families. A promise that, regardless of which teacher your student gets, all the teachers will do whatever it takes for your student to be successful. Unfortunately, this doesn't always happen. The key here is to have an ongoing commitment to strive to make this promise for every family. What striving for this promise means is that it matters who your teacher is. I am sure each of you can think of a teacher or two who has made a lasting difference in your life. They most likely held you accountable to high expectations, would do anything they could to support you, and you knew they believed in you. I am sure you can also recall a teacher or two who did not positively impact you. Mattos has always said schools must be able to make this promise to their families— regardless of your teacher, every child will get the support they need to be successful. Committing to a promise for every child is the first step in achieving certain access within your school.

Opportunities

♦ Acknowledge students will have different supports for assignments, and, as educators, we need to be okay with that. Not only be okay but encourage differences within our classrooms. Promote high expectations for all, but provide endless options for students to demonstrate their learning. Eliminate the talk in your building that it is unfair to provide students with different accommodations. Adults within the system need to understand and be okay with fair not always being equal.

◆ Develop a wide variety of accommodations for students. Accommodations can mean many things, from different ways for students to demonstrate their learning, length of time for completion of tasks or environmental changes. It is also possible to provide student accommodations in the process of reading. Reading accommodations allow more students to access grade level and beyond material by adjusting the cognitive load from the act of reading to higher order thinking skills, an accommodation that is very underutilized.

◆ Leaders should support teachers as they navigate individual student needs. Individualizing for every student is essential, yet very challenging, to accomplish. Collaboration is imperative for teachers to develop individualized plans to meet all learners' needs as much as possible. Leaders need to ensure teachers have time to collaborate and plan for differentiation. Do teachers have what they need to support students when they need it?

◆ Ensure that there is a fair and objective way to determine student academic needs, monitor academic progress, and implement support systems that serve all students. What data is used to drive instructional decisions about students? Is it consistent across grade levels and content areas? Are teachers using data to make instructional decisions about students? We need to support one another to move beyond gut feelings about kids and do our best to measure student performance. Data is one tool that can be utilized in this area. Why? Because people sometimes have perceptions that do not reflect what is actually happening in the school community.

◆ Support the development of a system of support that is responsive to student needs. To increase student performance in the classroom, assist teachers in engaging students in the appropriate support. Additional resources and supports do not create an equal classroom. They do, however, create a more equitable environment. Students with the most significant needs receive more support.

Equity of access is about providing opportunities and supporting students to engage in learning. The school's traditional practices can significantly inhibit the system's ability to respond to student needs when they need it. Reflecting on current practices helps us to find ways of increasing opportunities for all kids. It is hard to reflect and acknowledge our weaknesses, mistakes, and areas of growth. Continuous improvement is challenging work.

My challenge to all of us is not to become complacent in disparity. Do not continue to operate as you always have simply because that is how it has always been done. Challenge yourself and your colleagues. Challenge your colleges to look at how we can support kids differently. Examine your beliefs. Do your behaviors align with your beliefs? Is there one opportunity listed that you can use in your school or classroom?

Here's the best news about ensuring we are not only opening the door for students and supporting them to walk through it—we are not in this alone. No one person, teacher or leader, has all the strategies needed to support every student. Not one person has all the right answers. It truly does take a village. Continue to remain student-centered in all decisions impacting kids, and you will be successful in ensuring equal opportunity and clearing a path for all kids. Take advantage of the incredible opportunity educators have each day, to make a difference in the lives of students.

Resources

Belden, C. (2017, July 27). Equity vs. Equality: What Does Access Really Mean? The Inclusion Solution. Retrieved from www.theinclusionsolution.me/equity-vs-equality-access/.

Blankstein, A.M. and Noguera, P. (2016). *Excellence Through Equity: Five Principles of Courageous Leadership to Guide Achievement for Every Student*. Alexandria, VA: Association for Supervision & Curriculum Development.

Buffum, A., Matteos, M. and Weber, C. (2011). *Simplifying Response to Intervention: Four Essential Guiding Principles*. Bloomington, IN: Solution Tree Press.

Buffum, A., Matteos, M., Weber, C. and Hierck, T. (2015). *Uniting Academic and Behavior Interventions: Solving the Skill or Will Dilemma*. Bloomington, IN: Solution Tree Press.

Gamoran, A., Nystrand, M., Berends, M. and LePore, P.C. (1995). An Organizational Analysis of the Effects of Ability Grouping. *American Educational Research Journal*, *32*(4), 687–715. https://doi.org/10.3102/00028312032004687

Gay, G. (2010). *Culturally Responsive Teaching: Theory, Research and Practice*. New York, NY: Teachers College Press.

Griner, A.C. and Stewart, M.L. (2013). Addressing the Achievement Gap and Disproportionality Through the Use of Culturally Responsive Teaching Practices. *Urban Education*, *48*(4), 585–621. https://doi.org/10.1177/0042085912456847

Howard, T. and Terry Sr, C.L. (2011). Culturally Responsive Pedagogy for African American Students: Promising Programs and Practices for Enhanced Academic Performance. *Teaching Education*, *22*(4), 345–62. https://doi.org/10.1080/10476210.2011.608424

Larson, K.E., Pas, E.T., Bradshaw, C.P., Rosenberg, M.S. and Day-Vines, N.L. (2018). Examining How Proactive Management and Culturally Responsive Teaching Relate to Student Behavior: Implications for Measurement and Practice, *School Psychology Review*, *47*(2), 153–66. https://doi.org/10.17105/SPR-2017-0070.V47-2

Rosenthal, R. and Jacobson, L. (1968). Pygmalion in the Classroom. *The Urban Review*, *3*, 16–20. https://doi.org/10.1007/BF02322211

Shearer, E. (1967). The Long-term Effects of Remedial Education. *Educational Research*, *9*(3), 219–22. https://doi.org/10.1080/0013188670090309

Wagner, M., Newman, L., Cameto, R. and Levine, P. (2006). *The Academic Achievement and Functional Performance of Youth with*

Disabilities: A Report of Findings from the National Longitudinal Transition Study–2 (NLTS2). Menlo Park, CA: SRI International.

Vermeer, T.J. (2017). *Impacts of MTSS on the Performance of Struggling Students* [Master's thesis Northwestern College, Orange City, IA]. Retrieved from http://nwcommons.nwciowa.edu/education_masters/16/.

5

An Intersection in Our Educational Lives
We Are more than Meets the Eye

Oman Frame

> As a classroom community, our capacity to generate excitement is deeply affected by our interest in one another, in hearing one another's voices, in recognizing one another's presence.
>
> bell hooks (2017)

We are more than our first impression. When you meet someone, you see them, if you can; you hear their voice, if you are able; and you create a picture of them that is built piece by piece. Like a puzzle. The complete picture of ourselves is crafted with many layers of intersectional identity. Thank you, Kimberlé Crenshaw.

The concept of intersectional identity, and systemic and individual oppression impact our interpretation of every moment we spend in a community. We process ourselves in a constantly changing and shifting rotation of identity.

This chapter will begin the process of unpacking the multiple and dynamic identities that make up our experiences, as well as how those identities together create our worldview. This chapter will also begin the process of introducing the work of Kimberlé Crenshaw and how it applies to our classrooms and schools.

Part 1: How Does Intersectionality Show Up?

Often in the work of education, we play a bit of "oppression Olympics". Who is more oppressed—those whose marginalized identity falls into the category of race, gender, socioeconomic status, ability, religion, sexual orientation, weight, etc.? There is not just one identifier that matters. As students and teachers, we are all of these things, and the impact of certain identities shift within the context of all of our interactions. When microaggressions occur, they are often multilayered and how deep they cut depends on your lived experience (Sue & Spanierman, 2020). The life you live is often so multifaceted and layered that choosing one identity is redundant. One cannot choose which is more important; Black women cannot disconnect their gendered experience from their racialized experience and so on (Crenshaw, 2017).

This shows up in the classroom in a multitude of ways. As teachers, we parse the identity of our students into so many different categories that identity multiplies many times over. As teachers, it is our duty to liberate our students' opportunities and make spaces for them to be authentically themselves. Whole. Adding academic ability, behavior, extrovert versus introvert, linguistic style/code, and many more, often create such a dynamic and perfect picture of humanity. Our bias and internalized oppression lead us to be more conscious of difference and our response tends to be predicated on our experiences. Our affinity bias works toward our acceptance of students based on our shared experiences and their confirmation bias allows them to connect with us when we allow them to see parts of themselves in us as educators. The classroom is also riddled with disenfranchised opportunities. Stereotype threat is a real part of the education process in our world today. This all flows into the way intersectionality and identity politics play out. If you are an academically bored child, you may be seen from a deficit perspective. If you can "play the game" of education, you often find ways to accentuate yourself in spaces that may not be value-driven with certain identities. It plates out in minoritized experiences, such as "model minorities", gendered bias, and having to overcome obstacles (by one's bootstraps).

Part 2: Why Use an Intersection Lens?

In a world that is constantly changing in ways that affirm our multidimensional identities, we as educators must be on the cutting edge of identity development. We must see our students and colleagues for their entire identity. The intersectional lens should focus on the many parts of our whole, and highlight things that directly impact certain identities when engaging in both academic and social school work. For example, an intersectional approach to race in the classroom does not only focus on the racialized aspect and lived experiences of the students and teachers, but it also uses the focused identity (race) as an overarching theme and applies the other identities to its examination. Women who are Black, Indigenous or a Person of Color (BIPOC) would have a narrative that is affirmed from the perspective of both race and gender, and this process would back out across as many of the identities as possible, but would still be tethered to the concept of how race would impact them. The same process would apply to each of the other identities, and the format would allow the teacher to tailor the lesson to fit the identity of the students in front of them.

The intersectional approach would allow the community to validate the whole person, as well as keep the focus on certain aspects of our social world that rise to the forefront of our world. Intersectional work is the next phase of true inclusive classrooms. By understanding the multidimensional and multilayered students in front of you, it allows you to tailor lessons to play on the internal knowledge of themselves, as well as the application of their identity in lessons. As educators, it is our job to see our students within our systems of teaching and learning. When we set the stage for them to unpack their identity and find avenues for their identity to fit within their classrooms, we encourage multipoint engagement on the most important lessons.

This process is applicable in each discipline, and across grades and academic ability. When the whole child is engaged, when the intersectional lesson is presented and honored, the students will step up to the raw academic challenges because the needs of their identity will have been met.

The other part of the why we add more to the diversity, equity, and inclusion journey is, because the more we invest in the multidimensional lives of our students and ourselves, the more we reach all the students in front of us and learn more about how they learn best.

Intersectionality in the classroom is one of the most pivotal parts of the learning environment. When we feel seen, heard, and felt as a student we choose to be more invested and more involved in the learning process. Oftentimes those teachers with whom we connect validate our existence on many different levels. Our race; our gender; our religion or faith; our sexual orientation, or perceived sexual orientation; our ability/disability are all important aspects of how we see ourselves in the classroom and how we feel seen in the classroom. Intersectionality is a difficult part of the learning process simply because it takes time. That time invested upfront in the learning process or in the process of getting to know your teacher or class often yields far more learning and advances later down the line. Other aspects of the learning model which are enhanced by an intersectional approach are oftentimes the areas where our identity doesn't necessarily overlap but is our area of weakness or challenge. For example, if you are a person of color and you happen to be of a low socioeconomic status, there may be times when someone sees one of these identities as a detriment and does not see the benefits. The assets that can be there (i.e. community involvement, resilience, and task orientation, as well as determination and fortitude) are often overlooked. The complete and intersectional identity removes the burden of those "shortcomings" in a society that may not see them as important. Intersectionality also makes you multidimensional. We need to be more inclusive in our approach to understanding how we can involve more of our students' identities in this process all the time. The why to this conversation is always to increase the awareness of our blind spots, as well as of our areas of privilege. Often we don't have the language or lexicon to discuss these areas of privilege and oppression, but once we have the language or once we have a way of talking about them, the demystification process across differences becomes not only easy but beneficial to all. When this occurs, ownership of one's privilege can lead to reconciliation. The process is predicated on the people involved opening up and putting their privileges out there and learning to listen to the experiences in a validating way. An example would look like White students feeling compelled to be involved in a conversation on race, acknowledging how their privileged stance may create distance, men being compelled to involve themselves and understanding their position of privilege in a conversation of perceived gender, cis people in conversations about/with trans/intersex people, etc. Once privilege can be acknowledged and

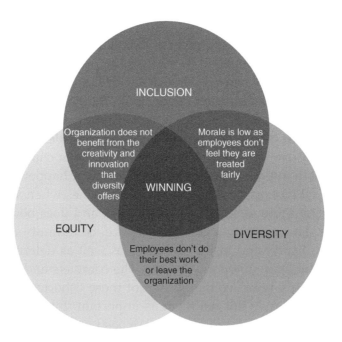

FIGURE 5.1 The Intersection of Equity, Diversion, and Inclusion.

© Turner Consulting Group. Used with Permission. www.turnerconsultinggroup.ca

set aside, the perspective can shift. By doing this, space can open up and allow for powerful dialogue and learning. In the classroom, it may allow for stereotypes to be dismissed, and also not reinforce a feeling of guilt or a helpless marginalized identity.

Part 3: When It Is Done Right

Many schools have diversity, equity and inclusion (DEI) programming and officers who are charged with creating and cultivating these efforts in a system that at times can see it as an add-on to the learning process. Many of these schools and school systems with DEI focus see their students in a more complete way. The DEI section of most schools' administration or hierarchy needs to be consistently moved both vertically and horizontally. It needs to be moved vertically up the chain of responsibility and responsibilities last command, as well as penetrating across horizontal lines to all areas of the grade level and also the division-level dynamic. Some heads of school or principals have said that diversity is not a one-off or a subcontracted space but it is more of one in which everyone should be engaged daily. Doing the work themselves or doing the work as a faculty or community on an individual basis raises the collective consciousness, which in turn raises the ability for all students to feel like their needs are being met. This is not a situation in which we are taking the load off, but more of a situation where, as a school, we are seeing kids for who they are—complete—and we are able to offer spaces where they can shine and learn in environments that celebrate them across many levels, not just an individual aspect of their identity.

When it is done right, schools thrive in many different dimensions (Hooks, 2017). When is done right, kids feel that they have multiple places to go when they are feeling like they need support; kids are open to hearing constructive criticism, knowing that the lenses that they are being seen through are as transparent as possible; and also when it is done right, you have buy-in across all identity spheres. You're talking about a space where kids of color feel seen for their racial identity, as well as kids who are in different ability spaces feel seen for their contributions to the learning environment. And, at the same time, all those things are interlocked, interlaced, and overlapped on top of each other, which just shows the gifts that we all bring to the table from many different perspectives. When it is done right, you have a coalition of people and not one or two people who are the experts. When it is done right, you also have a group of people who have really committed themselves to not only the learning process but also ensuring that the community grows socially, emotionally, as well as academically. When it is done right, the activities that are part of the DEI curriculum are interlaced once again with the learning outcomes and objectives across multiple disciplines. It is not just a humanities activity; it becomes a science activity, a math activity, a physical education activity, science activity, etc.

Applications

There are different types of applications in which intersectionality or the use of multiple identities would create a dynamic classroom (Hill Collins & Bilge, 2019). One of the most powerful ways is by centering one identity and then adding the others as additions to enhance the experience of the students in front of you. As an educator, you are going to present yourself in class with multilevel identities. By establishing good language around identity, you will create a unique learning outcome where a central part of your students' identity is going to be highlighted and other identities are going to create secondary and tertiary components of the learning process (Hooks, 2017). For example, say you are teaching a writing assignment in which the character had to be centered around race as their primary identifier, and their gender and socioeconomic status, and ability status, were also key components. Race would start the discussion, but as the character was developed, the other areas would have to shine through as well. In a rubric form, this could be used simply by the students knowing they had to show multiple identities of their character as they were writing this fiction or nonfiction piece. The same could go with a problem in social studies or history in which an expository essay was written by reflecting a time period. That focus, directly on looking at the role that gender played and then the secondary and tertiary role of the working class or affluent bourgeoisie, as well as the racialized component, allows the teacher and students to understand that marginalization plays out differently and in many different layers. It also would play out easily in other non-western societies, simply because to make the identities complete you'd have to take a much broader stance. To make them complete, you have to do your research in the workaround, understanding your community or the historical era that you are studying. It continues to move at that point. One of the other components of having race, gender, socioeconomic status, or ability status as a primary identity allows a multidimensional approach to the experiences being shared in the classroom (Hill Collins & Bilge, 2019). It embodies the intersectional approach and creates a space of belonging.

Below are some examples of the ways in which some of these main ideas can lead the discussion but are also made more powerful by opening the door to the other aspects of the identity spectrum that come into play. I would also highly recommend that the activity that leads the lesson be the social identity wheel. The social identity wheel allows kids and students, or any facilitated group, to prioritize their identity and not leave parts of themselves out of the conversation. There are many different versions of the social identity wheel, but one of my favorites can be found here: https://sites.lsa.umich.edu/inclusive-teaching/sample-activities/social-identity-wheel.

Race+

When engaging in educational opportunities for multiple identities are to be used, there are always additional components of the conversation. In this section, we are going to explore how the addition of race is a critical aspect of how we embody the intersectional process. Race+ takes place at the center of the conversation and learning environment, and at the same time allows for the other dimensions of our identity to be constructed within the range of the conversation. When you center race you start with something that the western world has propped up to begin the discussion on "diversity." Most institutions think diversity is centered around race and racial interaction. When we acknowledge that race is a central part of the intersectional arena, we validate and add to the complexity of our interactions.

Gender+

A very similar scenario is set up when you begin the focus of identity development with the gendered/binary identity at the forefront. When we start with this central identity, the stereotypes that accompany it can overshadow the other major identifiers. If you are of a marginalized gendered identity (i.e. trans, female) and a marginalized racial identity, your gendered experience is tainted and informed by this combination and the oppression hierarchy. By understanding and allowing for these variables to inform the way we interact with the students, and ourselves, it emphasizes the gendered experience and also combines the other identities as variables within the learning environment. This format allows for the study and exploration of identity with gender being the lead.

Class+

Once again, when you center the experiences of the economically marginalized population and the experience you create, pathways for those identities to show how they overcome the economic disparities often linked with working-class citizens appear. It is also a way to highlight the strength in areas that do not always make light within an economically-stratified society. If you can have a direct and open discussion of the way socioeconomic status shows up in your class and school, you will be opening the door to real inclusion and belonging. When socioeconomic class is highlighted, it gives paths to understanding the way even the most privileged can still be brought into the margins, and thus the commonality within groups is exposed. Class privilege is one of the most important aspects of the identity circle, and one that is inextricably linked to both race and gender.

Ability+

Often the most underrepresented part of our identity is our ability status. Within the DEI realm of academic understanding, one's ability, either physical or mental, is a key contributor to how fully invested in the learning process they can be. If students lead with areas of challenge, either physically or mentally, they open the door for vulnerability and empathy in the academic setting. By demystifying their disability, they turn the focus on the areas of strength and allow for better collaboration within the community. It allows for the acknowledgment of differences and also the areas where their strengths can shine. As stated in the other areas of "difference+", when we lead with these identities being given the attention that acknowledges challenges, they become areas where the learning environment is not predicated on marginalization, rather in the ability of strength in overcoming/surviving in a world of systemic oppression.

When a classroom is intersectional, or when we see our students as multifaceted and multidimensional human beings, we can adjust our lens and teaching style to smooth the rough spots of marginalization and truly get the most out of them. When we shift our teaching to be inclusive and culturally relevant to the areas of marginalization, we see them as whole humans who don't need to be fixed. We can meet them in the spaces in which they are both confident and fearful. By acknowledging our own intersectional identities, we also give them a blueprint for understanding how to navigate the shifting lenses of the school space. It is also critical that we use the areas of privilege in our identity to make spaces for those who are marginalized to find access and boost their access to education. The systemic nature of education often wants us to focus on the individual experiences and stay on track within the confines of subject and scores. I would suggest that we shift this paradigm to take the whole community and intersectional identities into consideration when looking at our pedagogy. If we can put aside the biases we have come to see as normal, we will truly open doors for all students and support those who need it the most. By doing this, we create a system of belonging, valuing all students and families as valuable members of the school community.

Conclusion

The reality is in a perfect world, we would be able to see our intersectional lives for what they are: Complete, engaging, and equal. Right now at the time of the COVID-19 summer of revolution, identity and the reality of our diverse and pluralistic society have made this aspect of our education system imperative. Our identity and practices around learning about it have to be bold. Identity has to live upfront and we, as teachers, have to be willing to be vulnerable, to take the risk of sharing who we are on every level (Hooks, 2017; Crenshaw, 2017). We must be able to listen and learn from others who see the world differently than we see it ourselves. Affinity is an amazing part of this process because it reminds us of the areas in which we shine and the area is growth that we have. It is important that in an intersectional world, each one of these things that make us who we are is constantly refreshed and discussed. It's the initial activities that allow us to see our communities' racial identity, our communities' nonbinary gender identity, our communities' socioeconomic status, or our class identity. It's another big component to making sure that we are aware of these things and that these are not taboo topics. We can have conversations in which we get a little uncomfortable and learn in an intersectional world, our race and our gender are commingled as well as our class, our ability status, or our religion. In an intersectional world, uncomfortable conversations lead to a deeper understanding of the way people in our community exist. That means that there are conversations around race that are truly eye-opening to privileged groups in America. What we can do when we go through this process together of becoming more intersectional is we can see each other for the complexity, as well as for the gifts, that we bring to a room that is not all homogeneous, and we can unlock the doors between us by just understanding each other, by just hearing each other's realities and putting them in a place that is both important to learn and listen, as well as important to express and exist. In doing this, we end up sharing our pain and we can heal through others' understanding.

The future of learning is in an equal and inclusive space. It is for us to open up and be vulnerable about our identity, not to sit aside. In this process of education, we must decide how we are going to see our students and our community. As long as we continue to work to see the multidimensional existence of others, we will be able to turn the corner on understanding how intersectionality truly makes us dynamic and truly allows for oppression to be measured at a rate that is inclusive of the multitiered experiences of multimarginalized people and groups.

Resources

Association for Women in Science. (2020). A Critical Framework for STEM Equity. Retrieved October 14, 2020, from www.awis.org/intersectionality/.

Coaston, J. (2020). The Intersectionality Wars. *Vox*. Retrieved October 13, 2020, from www.vox.com/the-highlight/2019/5/20/18542843/intersectionality-conservatism-law-race-gender-discrimination.

Crenshaw, K. (1989). *Demarginalizing the Intersection of Race and Sex: A Black Feminist Critique of Antidiscrimination Doctrine, Feminist Theory and Antiracist Politics. University of Chicago Legal Forum, 1989*(1). http://chicagounbound.uchicago.edu/uclf/vol1989/iss1/8.

Crenshaw, K. (2017). On Intersectionality: Essential Writings. New York, NY: The New Press.

Goodman, E. (2019). *How bell hooks Paved The Way For Intersectional Feminism. them*. Retrieved October 13, 2020, from <www.them.us/story/bell-hooks.

Hill Collins, P. and Bilge, S. (2019). *Intersectionality*. Durham, NC: Duke University Press.

Hooks, B. (2017). *Teaching to Transgress: Education as the Practice of Freedom*. Routledge/Dev Publishers & Distributors.

Sue, D.W. and Spanierman, L. (2020). *Microaggressions In Everyday Life, 2nd Edition*. Hoboken, NJ: Wiley.

6

Equity in Grading and Assessment

Jeffrey Zoul

For many years, I taught middle school and high school English. Harper Lee's classic novel, *To Kill a Mockingbird*, was a book we frequently read and studied. At one point in the novel, the main character, lawyer Atticus Finch, states that, in America, our courts must serve as the "great levelers" of society (Lee, 2006). By this, he means that all human beings should be equal before the law, and courtrooms, therefore, should not take into account a person's education, economic status, intelligence, or any other factor when deciding their guilt or innocence.

Of course, in the novel, unfortunately, justice is anything but blind and an African American man is unjustly found guilty in an Alabama courthouse. Although a work of fiction, the events in the novel reveal a truth of society both then and now: Our justice system is imperfect and at times innocent people are found guilty, while guilty people are set free. Still, the noble analogy of our justice system as a great leveler must remain the standard for jurisprudence in America. However, as important as it is for our courts to serve as "levelers" in our society, it is even more important that our schools serve as such. Because, while many citizens at some point in their lives may indeed find it necessary to seek justice in a court setting, many more, if not all, citizens enroll in school for an education and it is there that they must receive "educational justice," not only an *equal* opportunity to succeed, but also *equitable* treatment as a learner throughout their educational journey. It is important that our courts level the playing field for citizens seeking justice; it is critical that our schools do the same for all their students.

If our schools and classrooms are to serve as "great levelers" in our society, they must be places in which equity is not merely an esoteric virtue, but a non-negotiable commitment with concrete examples of actionable practices to be implemented. When discussing "equity" in education, we often think of "equality," but the former means *giving every person the same* while the latter means *giving every person what they need* to succeed. At its essence, "equity" is simply that: Giving every student what they need in order to succeed and fulfill their highest potential as a learner and citizen. Much like our justice system, we have come a long way in our schools to create learning environments that are both more "equal" and more "equitable." Yet, as with our courts, our schools have many miles to go before we can claim victory in the fight for equity.

What does equity in education look like in practice and what are the primary challenges we face in ensuring equity for all students? In examining the myriad aspects of equity in education, some are blatantly pernicious. For example, although educators everywhere have lamented for years that one's zip code must not determine one's quality of education, the unfortunate fact remains that students growing up in impoverished neighborhoods are far less likely to attend high performing schools than children residing in affluent neighborhoods (Kim et al., 2013). Other challenges to equity in education are perhaps far less dramatic and even—at first glance, perhaps—innocuous. The good news is that these types of obstacles to school equity should be relatively easier problems to fix; they require little in the way of financial resources. However, although they may not require a shift in budgetary priorities, they often require a radical shift in terms of mindset. One such area requiring a shift in mindset for equity relates to our grading and assessment practices. Many of the traditional grading and assessment practices we have clung to in schools for far too long are irrelevant or even counterproductive to student learning. Worse still, many of these practices serve as barriers to ensuring equity. Ensuring that every student gets what he/she needs when it comes to grading and assessment is an urgent and important teaching and learning matter. To achieve equity in terms of grading and assessment, we must shift the way we think about many of our current practices. Below are three worth considering.

Rethinking Competition

I consider myself to be a competitive person, perhaps overly so. For most of my younger years, competition in my life took place primarily as a member of a team, participating in sports such as basketball, soccer, baseball, and football. The competition was twofold: As a team member, I certainly wanted to beat our opponents, but the more intense competition within me was actually *against* my own teammates. I wanted to perform better than them so that I could earn more playing time. In both forms of competition, there were going to be "winners" and "losers." One team would lose to another and one teammate would "lose" playing time to another. As I grew older, my participation in athletics turned to more individual pursuits, such as golf and tennis. As I did so, my thoughts about competition began to change. When I began my teaching career, I began playing tennis in an organized league. I was, at best, a mediocre tennis player and our team was comprised of players with widely varying levels of tennis proficiency. My best friend on the team was a terrible tennis player. Every time we competed against each other, I would win, typically by scores of 6-0, 6-1, or 6-2. Although he was my friend and our schedules allowed us to play regularly, I found myself not at all enjoying competing against him. There was another member of the team who was definitely better at tennis than I. In fact, every time we played, he would win, usually by scores of 6-3 or 6-4. Although I did not know him well and he lived in a different part of the city, whenever he was willing, I would do whatever it took to play against him. I really enjoyed competing against him in tennis.

As I said at the outset, I have always been extremely competitive and a person who always wanted to "win." In this case, however, my thoughts were much different: I actually *enjoyed* losing and *hated* winning. The difference? When I was winning, I was not getting any better. I was bored and played politely, even trying to lose a few points here and there. On the other hand, when I was losing, I was actually getting better at tennis. I was completely engaged in the game, getting pushed to my limits and expending every ounce of energy I had within me to see how well I could do in the match. The real competition was not against my opponent, but myself. My goal was not to win (I accepted that winning against him was unlikely), but to become a better tennis player. In this tennis experience, when I won, I did not become better, yet while losing, I was actually improving as a player. The competition was no longer about winning or losing, or me against another competitor; instead, it was about getting better and competing not against an opponent, but against myself: Trying to become better today than I was yesterday.

How does this relate to equity in terms of grading and assessment in our schools? I think there are several key points to ponder:

1. In schools, we are still in the habit of "sifting and sorting" kids, often by using grades and assessments to identify student "winners" and student "losers." Although I think it is fine to have winners and losers when it comes to sports (particularly when the Chicago Cubs win and whoever they are playing loses), this is *not* acceptable in our classrooms and schools.

2. Competition in education can serve as a pernicious or productive influence on student learning. When students are competing against each other for limited spots on a "team" (e.g. number of As on a test or entry into an exclusionary academic program), competition is an obstacle to equity; we are pitting students against students and our classrooms must not be places in which we do this. It may be acceptable in athletics, but it is wrong in

our classrooms. Competition can be productive, however, when we create situations that inspire students to compete against their own performance, trying to be better today than they were yesterday and having clear standards of excellence in place that they are trying to achieve, making progress toward each day.

3. As educators, we must challenge our students to perform at their very highest levels each day, offering tasks that push and inspire them to exert their personal best effort each day. Dan Pink (2010) talks about "Goldilocks tasks" or what I call finding the "challenge sweet spot." When we assign tasks that are too easy, kids will be bored; when we assign tasks that are too difficult, kids can become frustrated. We must find the "just-right" level of task complexity so that students are engaged in productive struggle in an effort to progress from where they are now on the learning continuum to where they need to be next. In my tennis analogy, the challenge sweet spot was losing by scores of 6-3 or 6-4. Had I been playing Serena Williams and losing every match 6-0, losing would have lost its appeal and been neither fun nor productive.

4. I never received a grade for my tennis performance and never took a test assessing my tennis performance. I did, however, receive lots of feedback, both from fellow players who observed me and via self-assessment, as I experimented with new techniques and adapted these based on how well they worked. In tennis, as in any academic subject, there were simply a variety of skills I needed to practice and improve upon. No grade or test was going to help me get better at these skills, but practice, experimentation, and feedback did make a difference. Some might argue that the official tennis matches we played each weekend served as my "tests" or "grades," but even here I would make two observations. First, to the extent that a tennis match was an "assessment," at least

it was an authentic performance assessment, a culmination of the skills worked on during practice transferred to a formal event requiring all skills to be performed comprehensively. Furthermore, although as with any sporting event, we did keep score during the matches, the learning did not end with a final grade, whether we won a match 6-4 or lost 6-1. Instead, we reflected on how we played, identifying things we did well during the match and things we would need to work on before our next event. In schools, when we assign grades and administer assessments, it behooves us to ensure these are authentic and performance based. We must also insist that the grade or assessment is not an *end* of the learning process, but a *part* of the learning process, followed by reflection, feedback, and additional practice of targeted skills.

Competition often gets a bad rap in schools. As with most concepts, the "thing" itself is neither good nor bad; instead, it is how we implement the concept or practice. Competition can be a very harmful thing that creates unjust and unfair outcomes when we establish systems in which kids are forced to compete against each other for a limited number of winning results. However, when we individualize the tasks we assign students and individualize the way we assess their performance, instilling within them a desire to become better than they were and to move from their current point A to their next point B, we are nurturing students who desire to continuously improve and get better so that they can become the best they can be. And that type of competition is simply giving every student what he/she needs to succeed. **Bottom line:** When we misuse grades and assessment, we are also likely to foster unhealthy and inequitable competition among students in which they are pitted against each other instead of simply competing with themselves to become more proficient in terms of mastering the knowledge and skills expected of them according to defined learning standards.

Rethinking Tracking and Enrichment Programs

For several years, I served as the assistant superintendent for teaching and learning at a small K–8 district in an affluent suburban area. Parents in this district tend to be highly invested in the education of their children. They volunteered in schools, participated in PTA meetings and events, and kept in close communication with their children's teachers and principals. Although these parents were quite involved at the school level, it was rare for parents to contact me, an administrator at the district level. However, each spring, it was inevitable that at least a dozen or so parents would indeed reach out to me requesting a meeting. These requests coincided with letters sent out each spring notifying parents whether their children had qualified for the gifted/enrichment program for the following school year. Inevitably, the phone calls I received were from parents whose children did not qualify for the program and ranged from rather upset to fully enraged. *Side note: This "gifted" program had been in place long before I arrived and we actually tried to do away with the program every year. It was not a program of which we were proud and actually had a difficult time defending, yet parents in this community fought hard to keep it in place.*

Dealing with angry parents is never fun, but I found it much more manageable when I believed in what we, as educators in the district, were doing in terms of teaching and learning. This situation was perhaps the only one in my career when I found myself trying to defend something which I did not truly believe was best for kids. Again, I am not proud of this, but feel compelled to be completely honest. We had an intricate scoring matrix in place which we used to determine eligibility for entrance into the program. To be fair to my predecessors, they had reached out to nationally known experts in the field to develop the most logical, comprehensive, and defensible matrix possible, using a variety of measurements to consider when determining enrollment in the program. Still, the matrix we used resulted in a composite score that was difficult to explain or defend. Moreover, "seats" in the program were limited; as a result, each year some students "made the cut" and others were excluded based on a few random points one way or the other on a scale. It was an unjust and unfair system. Moreover, it was simply unnecessary. Why is it that many schools (and/or parents) feel compelled to separate kids into gifted/talented/enrichment/advanced programs as early as kindergarten? This is ludicrous at best and educational malpractice at worst, and we must fight against the urge to identify students in this way.

Here are a few points to ponder when considering tracking and enrichment programs, and using grades and/or assessments to qualify students for such tracks or programs:

1. No matter how carefully we design any measures to determine entrance into or exclusion from a gifted program or advanced track, the criteria used are inevitably somewhat arbitrary. In some instances, students who score quite highly on cognitive tests and "get in" actually struggle in their daily academics for a variety of reasons. In other instances, students who perform poorly on cognitive and/or achievement tests but would perform just as well as any other student in the program are excluded from participating.

2. Perhaps there comes a time in a student's academic journey when choosing a "track" to follow may well be defensible (preferably, when the student is invested enough in his/her own learning to self-select such a track). If so, that time is certainly not kindergarten. In fact, I would argue that no such programming should exist in any form at grades K–8. The earlier we allow "gatekeeper" classes and programming to exist in schools, the earlier we close doors to future options for students. We should be in the business of opening, not closing, doors to the future for all kids. Moreover, the earlier we do this, the earlier kids get the message that being "smart" is something you *are* instead of something *you can get*. We should be sending the message that "being smart" is something all kids can get, not just a select few. Even very young children are insightful and pick up on unspoken messages they receive in their classrooms. When we have

exclusionary gifted programs in place at early grades, you will hear students not in the program calling those in the program the "smart" kids. It is shameful when we create conditions at the elementary school level in which students begin to perceive themselves as not smart or not as worthy as some of their classmates.

3. These exclusionary advanced programs—particularly in early grades—often seem to be as much for parents as they are for students. And they seem to be as much about status as they are about meeting academic needs of included students. In districts where I served, some parents would spend significant amounts of time and money having their children "prep' for the assessments used to gain admittance into these programs. A few parents would stop at nothing to get their child enrolled in our enrichment programs—programs that often consisted of an hour or two each week of "pullout" services in which a few children from each classroom at a specific grade level would be removed from the regular classroom for rather vague learning enrichment activities. Inevitably each year, there would be at least one savvy parent who realized that the infrequent pullout programming was doing more harm than good and would remove their child from the program.

4. To show just how arbitrary entrance into gifted programming can be, a child who is identified as "gifted" in one school district can suddenly become "ungifted" when they move to a different district, since each district typically has its own measures and requirements for qualification—or perhaps has no such program in place at all. Even within districts, I have seen some children meet the requirements one year and fail to meet the requirements the following year.

5. In several schools where I served, these programs were referred to as being for "gifted and talented" students. I happen to think that all students are actually gifted and talented in one or more ways and most parents—not just the select few whose children participate—feel this way

about their own children. We need to shift our thinking when it comes to the concept of "talent" within our students, moving from "selecting" talent by identifying a few for special programs to "developing" the talent within every student.

The vast majority of student learning needs can and should be met in the regular education classroom. Separating kids for portions of the school day often results in unintended and counterproductive consequences, both for the students who leave the classroom for special programming and those who do not. Highly qualified and highly effective regular classroom teachers have both the desire and the ability to meet the needs of all students in their classroom, including students with varying levels of abilities in various subject areas. In some ways, such classrooms are not unlike my tennis experience. Most years, our tennis team consisted of 15 people possessing widely varying skill sets when it came to tennis. The leader of our team knew this full well and often partnered us with different teammates at practices and in matches. The groups we played in were dynamic and flexible, just as they should be in our classrooms. Some weeks, I was assigned to play in a singles match and other weeks I was assigned to play doubles. When playing doubles, my partner tended to change periodically, based on how well we performed together. Like any good classroom teacher, our tennis captain wanted each individual to perform at their optimal level each day and improve throughout the season and, as a result, placed us in positions to do so. He knew that for the team to be successful, each individual had to be successful. The same must hold true for schools: For a classroom to be successful, each student in the classroom must succeed. **Bottom line:** Creating exclusive enrichment tracks or programs promotes unjust and unfair educational opportunities, both within schools and across school districts. These programs set students apart from one another instead of bringing them together and entry into these programs is often based on arbitrary and even biased tests, grades, or teacher recommendations. They serve as a roadblock to educational equity.

Rethinking Practice and Feedback

The more often I played tennis, the better I became at tennis. Moreover, when I received specific, actionable feedback from fellow tennis players—particularly from a coach or player who had more tennis expertise than I—again, the more proficient I became. Human beings are learners by nature. We were born to learn and we learn in many ways, including the books we read, the people we meet, the places we go, and the experiences we have. However, two of the most critical ingredients to learning anything—from tennis, to guitar playing, to writing expository essays—are practice and feedback. In fact, for most things that we need or want to learn, they are essential and necessary components of the learning process. What are some things though that *are not* essential and necessary in order to learn something? Two come to mind right away:

1. Grades
2. Tests

In fact, I am not convinced that a grade has any influence on learning—except, possibly, a negative influence, since "bad" grades more often than not stunt, rather than enhance, learning. Of course, some assessments are helpful to the learning process, thus the idea that we have assessments for learning in addition to assessments *of* learning. But the vast majority of traditional assessments and standardized tests we use in schools are either irrelevant to learning or, worse, an impediment to learning. Our students can learn without grades or tests. Our students will not learn as much as they can, however, without deliberate practice and targeted feedback.

The idea that grades and testing are unnecessary for learning to occur is not a new one, nor, perhaps, is another fact related to traditional grades and standardized tests: They serve as a formidable obstacle to educational equity and a primary way we sift and sort students, creating academic winners and academic losers. Finally, it is also not a new idea that practice and feedback *are necessary* for learning to occur. Yet, in many schools, we continue to emphasize grades and testing and fail to provide enough time for students to practice the skills they need, offering them specific, actionable feedback along the way. I am actually *not against* an annual standardized test for all children. These tests can, indeed, offer a data point that provides us with some helpful information about a student. What I *am against*, however, is spending the rest of the school year focusing on and preparing for the annual test and using the results of such tests to limit learning opportunities for certain students based on their score on this one data point. In my tennis story, although there were no formal tests, the weekly matches against an opposing team were a type of "test." We need more tests like this in schools: Culminating projects, papers, activities, and events that require students to show what they know and can do by putting all the knowledge and skills they have acquired during a unit of study together into authentic evidence of learning. In tennis, there were also no formal grades, yet the practice I put in and the feedback I received let me know how I was progressing, as well as what I needed to work on prior to my next "test." We need to shift our thinking and practices in schools toward a performance model of grading and assessing kids. We must replace turning something in for a grade to expecting students to provide authentic evidence they have learned.

Here are a few additional points to ponder when rethinking how to prioritize practice and feedback over grades and testing:

1. Grades are often a reflection of student compliance as much as they are about student learning. A student who "does school well" in terms of behavior, attendance, turning in assignments on time, and completing homework regularly is likely to receive a good grade. On the other hand, a student who misbehaves, is absent frequently, and fails to complete homework is likely to receive a not-so-good grade. Yet, the possibility exists

that the student with the better grade is no more proficient in relation to the learning standards than the less compliant student with the crummy grade. In such cases, grades become less about learning and more about compliance.

2. Any time we discuss grades, we must also discuss points. In grading systems with "points," we inevitably—if inadvertently—again create student winners and losers. For students adept at playing the game who rarely miss an assignment, it becomes about chasing points—or *earning*, rather than *learning*. Students become point collectors instead of knowledge connectors. For students not inspired or motivated by points, it becomes an even less satisfactory game, with an even more harmful outcome: Zeroes and failing grades followed by placements in remedial programs and less rigorous tracks of study. In both instances, grades fail our students; at best, they motivate students to earn points. At worst, they cause students to lose hope. In neither case do they motivate students to pursue learning.

3. In terms of standardized testing (as with most aspects of education), I do not believe in absolutes and am hesitant to suggest we should never employ these. Used judiciously, they can serve as but one way to assess cognitive ability and achievement levels. However, we must recognize that many standardized tests are limited and, worse, biased. For instance, students whose parents have more education and/or higher incomes tend to perform better on the tests (Goldfarb, 2014). Test scores are also racially biased, with Whites and Asians scoring better than Blacks and Latinx (Reeves & Halikias, 2017).

4. In the past two decades, I have had the good fortune to observe thousands of educators teaching at all grade levels and in every possible subject area. Over time, I discovered something consistent about the performing arts (chorus, band, dance, and orchestra) and physical education lessons I observed; they tended to include frequent cycles of:

practice – feedback – additional practice

In these lessons, students perform a skill (they sing, play an instrument, dribble a basketball) while the teacher listens and watches. At some point, the teacher tells the student(s) to stop and provides specific feedback on what they noted about the performance. Then, the student(s) try again, almost always with a slightly better result than the previous attempt. This strikes me as a much more natural and effective learning cycle than its more frequent counterpart consisting of:

Student passively receives information, at some point student takes a test on the information, eventually student receives an overall grade based on the test and other assessments, unit of study ends and they move on to the next unit of study.

The more we can replace cycles of learning dominated by grades and testing with those comprised of frequent practice and feedback, the more our students will learn. In addition, the more we can "coach" our students as opposed to "teaching" academic content, the more invested all learners will become in their own learning. **Bottom line:** Grades and standardized tests are not always valid and reliable methods of determining how much a student has learned. Moreover, traditional grading and assessment practices can be imprecise, demotivating, and even biased, benefiting some students while harming others. They are potential roadblocks to educational equity. On the other hand, providing opportunities for *all* students to engage in deliberate practice, followed by personalized, specific feedback, helps to create a level playing field in which students know what the learning goal is, where they currently are in relation to the goal, and what they must do next to move forward along their personal learning continuum.

Rethinking the Purpose of Grades and Assessments

For a few years, I left public education and worked full time as a consultant and school improvement specialist for a non-profit organization. During those years, I worked for a boss who often said, "What's best for the best is best for the rest." Although I was a tad uneasy with the saying because it implied some students are better than others, I wholeheartedly support the true sentiment behind his words based on our current reality. For far too long, we have maintained a system whereby we sift and sort kids, largely based on grades we assign and assessments we administer, neither of which are wholly defensible. This sorting of students results in long-term consequences for those identified as "less than the best" which can be limiting, if not damaging, to their learning and to their future far beyond the schoolhouse walls. The system is unjust and unfair. Kids who "win" get placed in challenging, rigorous programs of study, often taught by the best teachers in the school. Meanwhile, kids who "lose" because of the grades they receive or scores on a standardized test are assigned to a remedial track, which brings to mind another favorite saying of my former boss: We can never "remediate" a child up to grade level standards; we must *accelerate* them up to grade level standards. His overall point is well taken and rooted in fairness and equity: Whatever learning experiences we provide for our kids who are performing at high levels in school, we should also provide for every child in the school. To achieve equity, we must give every child what they need to succeed. What our "best" students need (and often receive) is what the "rest" need as well.

We must fight for equitable practices in our schools in many areas, from funding, to facilities, technology access, and in scores of other ways both large and small. Rethinking traditional grading and assessment practices cannot be overlooked when we are identifying current teaching and learning practices that create inequitable outcomes for students. To the extent that we need grades at all in our schools, the purpose of grades must be clearly defined and reiterated, and that purpose must be to communicate where a student is in relation to clearly defined learning standards at a given point in time. As far as assessment is concerned, outside of an annual standardized, accountability test, the primary purpose of ongoing assessment for learning should be to determine where a student needs to get to, where he/she is currently along the continuum toward that goal, and what the next necessary steps should be to get from here to there. To promote equitable learning outcomes, instead of focusing so much on grading and testing, perhaps we simply need to keep asking the foundational questions of any professional learning community (DuFour & Eaker, 2009).

1. What is it our students need to know and be able to do at each grade and in every subject?
2. How will we know if they know and can do what is expected of them?
3. How will we respond when some students do not learn?
4. How will we respond when some students have already mastered the intended learning?

Keeping these four core teaching and learning questions at the forefront of any conversation we have about any student's learning goals and progress toward these goals is a simple, if mundane, way in which we practice equity. They are also a way to fulfill the purpose of grades and assessment.

Toward a more Equitable System

When playing tennis, my foremost goal was simply to become better. And, whenever possible, I put myself in a position to become better. Of course, I also understood that when playing tennis matches, sometimes I would win and sometimes I would lose. In tennis—or any other athletic event—I am OK with that. I am not OK, however, with identifying winners and losers when it comes to the students we serve in our schools. We must ensure that the focus is on every student getting better every day and doing whatever it takes to achieve that goal. By eliminating competition among students while encouraging a competition within themselves to become better today than they were yesterday, we are more equitable. By eliminating programs of study that elevate some students while limiting others, we are more equitable. By subordinating in importance grades and tests in favor of practice and feedback, we are more equitable. And by starting with a clear understanding about the purpose of grades and assessment, and staying true to those purposes, we are more equitable.

In *To Kill a Mockingbird*, even though Atticus tells the jury that in the courts "all men are created equal," he knows that the prejudices of the people make this a far-fetched proposition (Lee, 2006). It is even more important that in our schools we believe and fight for our belief that "all students are created equal." Our schools must serve as the "great levelers" of society. As such, we must serve them with equity, giving each child what he/she needs to succeed.

Resources

DuFour, R. and Eaker, R.E. (2009). *Professional Learning Communities at Work: Best Practices for Enhancing Student Achievement*. Moorabbin, VIC: Hawker Brownlow Education.

Goldfarb, Z.A. (2014, March 5). These Four Charts Show How the SAT Favors Rich, Educated Families. The Washington Post. Retrieved August 2, 2020, from www.washingtonpost.com/news/wonk/wp/2014/03/05/these-four-charts-show-how-the-sat-favors-the-rich-educated-families/.

Kim, S., Mazza, J., Zwanziger, J. and Henry, D. (2013). School and Behavioral Outcomes Among Inner City Children: Five-Year Follow-Up. *Urban Education, 49*(7), 835–56. https://doi.org/10.1177/0042085913501895

Lee, H. (2006). *To Kill a Mockingbird*. New York, NY: Harper Perennial Modern Classics.

Pink, D.H. (2010). *Drive: The Surprising Truth about what Motivates Us*. Edinburgh: Canongate.

Reeves, R.V and Halikias, D. (2017, February 1). Race Gaps in SAT Scores Highlight Inequality and Hinder Upward Mobility. Brookings. Retrieved August 2, 2020, from www.brookings.edu/research/race-gaps-in-sat-scores-highlight-inequality-and-hinder-upward-mobility/.

7

Equity, Resilience, and...Chess

Salome Thomas-EL

The Case for Equity

Teachers and principals who work in our nation's schools have faced some major challenges in 2020. In March, they had to cancel in-person classes to contain the spread of the COVID-19 virus. The majority of those schools had to remain closed for the school year and provide remote learning opportunities at home for their students. While at home during the pandemic, those students witnessed a number of racial incidents, including the deaths of Breonna Taylor, Ahmaud Arbery, George Floyd, and several others. The deaths of these unarmed Blacks have sparked protests in 200 cities, in nearly 30 states. The marches and protests have forced us as a country, to take a closer look at the policies in our nation surrounding police brutality, social justice, equality, racism, and equity.

Equity in our schools has been a popular topic for the past several years and at the forefront of many debates in education on improving schools for all children, including those who live in poverty and struggling communities. Many education experts will argue that poverty prevents students from succeeding in school and life, but there are clear examples, supported by research, of students who, given the proper interventions, overcome the odds to live productive and successful lives. Equity in education would mandate that we create and develop programs in our schools that provide all children, regardless of their economic status, an equal chance for success. Although we know many poor and minority students struggle in school, those who have access to good schools that offer a rigorous curriculum with a safe and nurturing environment, high quality teachers, and after-school programs, are more likely to rise above their conditions (Williams & Anthony, 2015). Understanding the challenges and barriers our students face is the first step to supporting and helping them overcome these obstacles.

Positive Relationships

One of the keys to supporting students so that they become successful is to develop supportive schools that focus on building positive adult–child relationships. The presence of a caring teacher or adult in a school who displays an attitude of compassion and who provides support for a child—even when they exhibit negative behavior—establishes a healthy relationship that often leads to learning and success in school. Most educators know that all behavior from students is communication. Oftentimes their negative behavior is a way to express that they have experienced some level of trauma, and they are simply reaching out for love and relationships. Positive relationships with teachers give students the motivation and desire to succeed. Children will work hard and do things for people they love and trust (Williams & Anthony, 2015). Improving public schools so that they focus more on building relationships instead of focusing on increasing test scores, should be the vision and goal of every school district. On a daily basis our goal as teachers and leaders should be to ensure equity and make sure that every child has the opportunity and support to be successful.

The world has been a frightening place for our kids. Educators are consistently concerned about how they can support their students and help them remain calm as they witness the unrest and protests in our nation. Domestic terrorism and wars around the world, along with school shootings and crime in their communities, make life very stressful overall for teachers and students. Teachers are not able to protect their students from the trials and tribulations of life but they can give them the tools, resilience, and perseverance to cope with and overcome the many problems they will encounter. The fostering of resilience in adolescents can provide the skills needed to become successful in school and lead to a positive life. Resilient students are able to utilize their strengths to cope with problems and setbacks. Researchers defined resilience early on as the ability to "bounce back" after instability and trauma to lead a successful and productive life (Masten, 2013).

Often students in the poorest school districts across the country, in both city and rural areas, are forgotten by state and federal lawmakers. Although there has been some progress in a small number of schools and districts, the country continues to face a significant challenge in successfully educating our students who struggle most. Achievement is often lower for poor or minority students in most, if not all, urban and suburban school districts, and for many, the immediate response is to blame educators. This is not a very effective strategy. We need to be supporting teachers and equipping them with the tools and skills to help high needs students. And that is right after we begin to pay them more. There are a multitude of factors affecting student achievement, many of which impact students long before they ever attend school. However, if students are to become successful, they will need teachers who are caring and dedicated to improving their resilience and perseverance (Dixson, Royal & Henry, 2013). Understanding the cultural backgrounds of the students they serve is paramount for principals and teachers who wish to inspire and motivate our children who struggle most.

Resilience

Resilient students have distinct advantages when it comes to recovering from risks in life such as abuse, poverty, and lack of a supportive caregiver. The fostering of resilience in adolescents can provide the skills needed to become successful in school and lead to a positive life. If children are provided with the proper home, school, and community support systems at an early age, they are more likely to learn to cope with adverse situations and develop the resilience necessary to achieve better outcomes. Most often, that support takes place at school. District and school leaders must support the goal of equity for all by providing the resources and materials that teachers need, including training and professional development, to ensure that the needs of all students are met. Resilience helps to develop persistence, optimism, and hope within our students.

Schools can become sources of faith, hope, and optimism for students and their families. School leaders must prioritize focusing on developing school communities that are comfortable and intentional about celebrating the cultures and successes of all people. They must create ways to challenge the status quo to develop high expectations and supportive learning environments for all students. This consistent message of equity in education is an effective way to address what can be done at the individual school and classroom level, to create a more equitable environment for students. Children whose lives have been disrupted by significant challenges at home and in their communities need to experience love, care, and support in school.

Developing resilient youth and reducing the effects of adversity and trauma on children is essential to the care and support provided by any school community. Resilient children are able to sustain their self-worth and emotional well-being even in the face of adversity. They don't fear failure or struggle. When failure is taught to be a part of the path to success, resilience becomes second nature for students. Trauma-informed adults and strong family engagement are two common characteristics of supportive school communities. Resilience is believed to be influenced by the healthy relationships developed with parents, teachers, and other adults in the school building, along with involvement in extracurricular activities (Bowles & Pearman, 2017).

When children from disadvantaged communities are given opportunities to build their sense of self-worth through positive relationships in school and access to after-school programs, they learn to overcome life's obstacles on their own. These opportunities include the use of a variety of social-emotional skills, including empathy, kindness, and interpersonal communication. The opportunities afforded to at-risk youth create what social scientists call "protective factors", which protect students from negative influences that they otherwise would experience without school and community-based opportunities to succeed.

After-school programs that offer sports, recreation, and academic support expose children to positive influences and mentors who teach them how to positively interact with others. The literature on resilience in terms of the characteristics that act as protective factors focuses on the internal and external assets that help children overcome difficult life circumstances. A child with a sense of belonging who feels that they are treated fairly in their school begins to develop resilience at a young age and feels connected to the positive culture in the school (Masten, 2013). Teachers and principals can play a major role in building resilience in students by conveying an attitude of compassion, understanding, and respect for the student.

Teachers and mentors who offer trustworthiness, respect, and genuine interest in children often develop long-lasting relationships with students, which encourages them to learn, even when it may seem difficult. Often, the teacher is the most frequently encountered positive role model outside of the family. Many high poverty communities report struggling to keep good teachers in their districts, which poses a major challenge for schools facing equity issues. Over half of all students in our country who struggle in school come from disadvantaged homes and communities. These communities, which already deal with the negative impact of poverty, continuously face the daunting challenge of retaining high quality teachers.

The culture of the school is important also, as is the student's ability to feel supported, safe, and celebrated. It is necessary for schools to provide opportunities for students to have their accomplishments and successes celebrated. Positive school and community cultures are important to a student's self-efficacy, self-esteem, and resilience. Students learn important social and problem-solving skills in schools that promote positivity, academic achievement, and extracurricular activities.

Lessons Learned Early in My Teaching Career

I began my teaching career in 1987 in north Philadelphia, working in a very impoverished community very similar to the community where I lived as a young man raised by a single mom. With my roots in the housing projects and public housing in the inner city, I knew immediately that I would have to develop powerful relationships with those young students to help them realize the resilience and persistence that they possessed. Their dedication to becoming successful, even without father figures, was impressive. I knew that all they needed was a level playing field and the ability to overcome their obstacles, to advance beyond a community riddled with violence, drugs, and crime. I needed a game changer for those students, a great equalizer!

In 1994, I began a middle school chess program while teaching in the inner city of Philadelphia, where I met hundreds of young African American students, mostly boys, who were all fifth through eighth graders. They were students who were achieving excellent grades but appeared to be missing the critical ingredients needed to beat the odds and become successful in a troubled, high risk community. Students who find success in school and life rely on several protective factors, such as developing relationships with compassionate adults who may work in school or in the community, a structured home life, and supportive schools.

Students in our school and many other schools, lacked the critical thinking and problem-solving skills necessary to make good choices and life-changing decisions. The crime rate was very high in the neighborhood that surrounded Vaux Middle School where I taught, and we lost multiple teens to violent murders in our community. Schools in the inner city and in urban communities can face some severe challenges, including high rates of poverty, limited resources, excessive teacher turnover, increasing numbers of behavior issues, and less experienced or unqualified teachers. Not all inner-city schools face these issues, nor are these challenges limited to urban areas, but inner-city schools and urban communities share characteristics that are quite different from suburban school districts. All students should have access to a high quality curriculum that fits their educational needs, high quality teachers who are prepared to meet their needs, and the proper support to help them find success.

I learned early on in my career as a teacher that the road to success for students in the communities that were struggling the most was paved with education and support from school. In order to assist teachers and principals, urban schools would need to provide access to rigorous courses and after-school programs. To ensure the success of all students, schools would also have to become places that valued high standards, collaboration, communication, and data-driven decision-making. Students needed extended learning opportunities like homework assistance, chess, and STEM (science, technology, engineering, mathematics) programs.

Many African American and Latinx children deal with traumatic experiences regardless of their socioeconomic or community background so it is very important for them to develop in caring and supportive school cultures that embrace resilience (Williams & Bryan, 2013). The risks that many poor or minority students face can derive from under-resourced schools, family stress, or negative community interactions. The most underserved students need equitable school funding and access to the necessary resources to overcome the risks they face.

I decided to introduce some students to chess because of the values it teaches them and what it could do to improve their critical thinking skills, self-efficacy, resilience, and outlook on life. I needed to find a way to inspire these young men and women to believe that they could overcome the obstacles in their neighborhood and improve their resilience. Our girls, who went on to become undefeated over multiple years, truly embraced the challenges of learning chess. It gave them a feeling of confidence and power knowing they could defeat any boy in the school—and any male teacher like me, too! I guess that's why the queen is so powerful. Chess has been acknowledged for quite some time as a builder of strong intelligence, and improving the cognitive abilities and rational thinking of young people (Bart, 2014). Participating in chess programs can influence logical thinking, self-confidence, and self-worth, and encourages students to appreciate the significance of perseverance, attentiveness, and commitment.

After-school programs and extracurricular activities influence the environments of adolescents, and have become a major part of the extended school day for children. Facilitating the social and emotional development of children has become the primary focus of these programs, and they are most effective when students meet on a regular basis throughout the school year, they are supervised by adults who they trust and respect, and are offered structured activities.

After-School Programs

Effective extracurricular activities improve academic achievement and provide a wide range of benefits to students. They can reduce at-risk behaviors, build self-esteem and resilience, and provide a nurturing and safe environment for young people. Students enrolled in extracurricular activities are more likely to develop positive relationships with adults, improve behavior, build more confidence, and take healthy risks. These behaviors are all associated with increasing self-esteem and self-efficacy. Often, students who struggle with behavior issues during the normal school day find success in extracurricular activities after school. According to most research, students are more likely to be involved in at-risk behavior or crime between the hours of 3:00 p.m. and 6:00 p.m., and after-school programs can prevent students from engaging in at-risk behavior during those hours, which potentially results in improved grades and fewer behavior problems.

Excellent after-school programs promote critical thinking, problem-solving, risk-taking, and make learning fun for students. One national study (Durlak & Weissberg, 2007) found that over 40% of students who attend after-school programs improve their reading and math grades. Extracurricular activities provide students with opportunities to gain resilience and experiences of self-efficacy. When the activities are as diverse as dance, student government, public speaking and debate, swimming, track, tennis, chess, music, band, and sports, they offer students opportunities to interact in a positive environment with other students and adults.

Children who are taught to think critically become adults who live caring and empathetic lives. Critical thinkers raise vital questions and problems, think open-mindedly, recognize problems, and assess consequences (Conklin, 2018). Twenty-first century skills such as critical thinking, problem-solving, and communication are vital for adolescents to succeed in school. Many teachers are mandated to focus instruction on testing and not critical thinking skills or other activities that stimulate brain development. Teaching students to take risks and become comfortable with making mistakes is how they develop a growth mindset. Extracurricular programs offer the perfect outlet for both social and intellectual development, especially during the middle school years.

Traditionally, children who live healthy and successful lives at home and school are exposed to positive relationships and interactions with adults when they are very young.

Negative interactions and traumatic relationships with adults affect the long-term success of students. There are opportunities in school for students to protect against the effects of traumatic experiences. Participating in after-school activities, like chess, help to develop the prefrontal cortex of the brain, which is responsible for cognitive development and decision-making. Most students don't improve their judgement and decision-making skills until they are teens or older. And boys develop these skills much later than girls. This makes chess an important game to play for adolescents (Garner, 2012). The problem is that not all children learn to play chess at home, which is why learning chess in school during extracurricular programs is so important. Chess is not only about problem-solving and cognitive development; it also provides a platform for players to enhance their persistence, also known as "grit." Angela Duckworth (2016), psychologist and researcher, defined grit as persistence, and perseverance to achieve long-term goals. Grit allows students to persist through tough times by giving them the character and passion to achieve their goals, even when their obstacles seem insurmountable.

Schools can develop grit in their students if they teach them to learn from their defeats while remaining positive. Teach them that struggling is a necessary part of the process to grow and learn. This creates a culture that supports resilience, self-esteem, and confidence. Providing enrichment activities and after-school programs allows students to discover their passions and personalize their learning activities (Dixson, Royal & Henry, 2013). Personalized learning cultures in schools is a major asset for achieving equity in all schools. In equitable schools and classrooms, all students are given the support they need to maximize their educational experiences. Activities that promote critical thinking and problem-solving, like chess, allow students to focus on specific skills that they find interesting and beneficial.

Building Equity Through Chess

Students who play chess in school programs, in the community, or at home benefit in many ways. Chess helps to develop the resilience, intellectual skills, and social development of adolescents (Bart, 2014). One of the largest benefits of participation in a chess program is the influence of the consistent interaction with children of all academic and cognitive abilities, which helps to improve the critical thinking and problem-solving skills of all students. Chess has been described as a game that is a distinctive relationship of two players who participate rationally and learn much from one another. Chess requires students to think critically and analyze on every move and has been found to increase the creative and mental abilities of children. The mental abilities developed through playing chess include memorization, reasoning, and concentration, and these skills are used in school and throughout life as an adult. Some of those skills include problem-solving, focusing, critical thinking, abstract reasoning, strategic planning, creativity, analysis, evaluation, and synthesis.

Chess as a school activity makes a very important contribution to the education and responsibility of young children through teaching them to take risks and understanding the consequences for their actions. Children develop courage from playing chess, and that courage enhances their grit and resilience. Often in chess, students learn more from losing games than they do from winning. Learning to accept losses with dignity builds confidence. When students become more confident and resilient, they are more likely to view their challenges and obstacles as temporary barriers to success (Garner, 2012). Children are often motivated to play chess, and even when they lose, they quickly develop persistence, grit, and perseverance.

Chess is an activity that exercises the mind and develops mental abilities, allowing players to embrace challenges and deal with failure, thus developing resilience that translates beyond the game. The game of chess is a very important teaching tool. In today's society, where teachers and parents battle with social media, the internet, and video games for the attention of children, chess teaches students to follow rules, focus on their school work, and concentrate on important issues that affect their success. Chess contains the basic principles of psychological learning theory, memory, pattern recognition, decision-making, and reinforcement. When students repeatedly make similar moves in games, they must memorize creative patterns and combinations on the chess board. When students improve their memories, it helps them in all academic areas in school, especially art and music.

Problem-solving, planning, reflecting, decision-making, and rewards and consequences, are the cornerstones of chess. When students learn to master the skills of chess, they determine that every move has several options and the ability to make decisions or choose the best option will determine their success in the game. Key skills such as problem-solving, critical thinking, and communication are major influences on a child's ability to succeed early in school (Conklin, 2018). Acquiring these skills would benefit our students of color who often face multiple academic and societal challenges each day and need to become more resilient.

Teachers who work in urban schools reported that students from supportive homes and those who participated in after-school programs, increased their self-confidence and self-esteem in the classroom and other aspects of the school. After-school programs that involve activities that promote critical thinking, like the game of chess, are believed to reinforce the educational skills students require to succeed in school. A major conclusion of many studies is that chess instruction improves the academic and cognitive ability, and resilience of students (Garner, 2012). The problem is not all schools are equipped with the resources to provide after-school programming to support programs like chess clubs, and more are needed so that the world can see the positive impact these programs have on students, especially male African American students who experience from low engagement with school more than any other demographic. Because of all the benefits associated with chess, it can become a vehicle for "hooking" our most at-risk students into staying—and succeeding—in school. Chess, in essence, can become a vehicle for academic equity.

Conclusion

Equity is hard work and there is no one in education who is passionate, knowledgeable, and committed, who will tell you anything different. But those same thoughtful and experienced educators will also tell you it is necessary work and the key to eliminating disadvantages for students in our schools. I chose to focus on resilience and chess, and its relationship to equity in this chapter because they are two concepts I chose to focus on in my career in education for over 30 years and that I have seen, firsthand, make a positive impact on students who need our support the most. Two-thirds of those years have been spent as a school leader, and I am still helping to lead the charge in this education revolution.

Chess impacts the ability of young people to reason and think critically, and forces them to become more patient and analytical. The development of 21st century skills will improve the chances for students to find success in school and life, and result in positive outcomes in youth who faced adversity. Many of the children in our school in Philadelphia who were exposed to chess at a young age overcome obstacles through resilience and perseverance.

Much of the research on resilience is focused on poverty and minority students, and that is a great first step because a disproportionate number of African American children live in communities inundated with violence, crime, drugs, and unemployment (Shabazian, 2015). We know that these children are exposed to high levels of trauma in high risk environments, and are more likely to experience academic and behavioral struggles. Establishing consistent levels of equity in schools and supporting every student, and not just students from disadvantaged backgrounds, but those from the suburbs and rural areas, will help to eliminate the risk factors that impact their success. Equity in schools will also help educators address the very important social-emotional development of students and improve the well-being of their school communities.

Many African American students do not believe the education system is designed for them to succeed and they often feel detached from their school environments. This was one of the primary reasons I wanted to start a competitive chess team in my school in the inner city. Many were surprised to see those students involved in the chess program become state and national champions, but I wasn't. I knew they had the drive and commitment to become the best and achieve their goals. Many of those students went on to college, graduate school, and law school. This chapter contains some key points that demonstrate how schools can become intentional about equity, building resilient students and teachers, and teaching critical thinking and engaging students to change their perceptions through the game of chess. After-school programs like chess challenge students and encourage them to develop grit and perseverance. Empowering our students to advocate for themselves is one of the many benefits of building an equitable school environment, along with ensuring the success of all students with diverse learning needs, including those enrolled in special education and English language learner (ELL) programs. Education for our students will be their saving grace, so we must ensure that all students receive the very best opportunities possible while in school. In my experience, building resilience through chess has been a great equalizer among the student populations I have served, becoming a game changer in terms of more equitable educational outcomes.

Resources

Bart, W. (2014). On the Effect of Chess Training on Scholastic Achievement. *Frontiers in Psychology, 5*(762). https://doi.org/10.3389/fpsyg.2014.00762

Bowles, F.A. and Pearman, C.J. (Eds.). (2017). *Self-efficacy in Action: Tales from the Classroom for Teaching, Learning, and Professional Development*. Lanham, MD: Rowman & Littlefield.

Conklin, H.G. (2018) Caring and Critical Thinking in the Teaching of Young Adolescents. *Theory Into Practice, 57*(4), 289–97.

Dixson, A.D., Royal, C. and Henry, K.L. Jr. (2013). School Reform and School Choice. In H.R. Milner IV and K. Lomotey (Eds.), *Handbook of Urban Education* (pp. 474–503). New York, NY: Routledge.

Duckworth, A. (2016). *Grit: The Power of Passion and Perseverance*. New York, NY: Scribner/Simon & Schuster.

Durlak, J. and Weissberg, R. (2007). *The Impact of After-School Programs That Promote Personal and Social Skills*. Chicago, IL: Collaborative for Academic, Social, and Emotional Learning.

Garner, R. (2012, November 10). Chess Makes a Dramatic Comeback in Primary Schools. *The Independent*. Retrieved from www.independent.co.uk/news/education/education-news/chess-makes-a-dramatic-comeback-in-primary-schools-8301313.html.

Masten, A.S. (2013). Risk and Resilience in Development. In P.D. Zelazo (Ed.), *Oxford Handbook of Developmental Psychology 2nd Edition* (pp. 579–607). New York, NY: Oxford University Press.

Shabazian, A.N. (2015). The Significance of Location: Patterns of School Exclusionary Disciplinary Practices in Public Schools. *Journal of School Violence, 14*(3), 273–98.

Williams, J. and Bryan, J. (2013). Overcoming Adversity: High-achieving African American Youth's Perspectives on Educational Resilience. *Journal of Counseling and Development, 91*(3), 291–300. https://doi.org/10.1002/j.1556-6676.2013.00097.x

Williams, L.R. and Anthony, E.K. (2015). A Model of Positive Family and Peer Relationships in Adolescence. *Journal of Child and Family Studies, 24*(3), 658–67. https://doi.org/10.1007/s10826-013-9876-1

8

Unapologetically Equitable in Action

Abdul Wright

Systems Do Not Create Equity. People Do

Abolish slavery. Desegregation. Achievement gap. School to prison pipeline. Equity. All terms. All phrases. You see, words—no matter how trendy—have an intended purpose, and the intended purpose is connected to a why. A why that is connected to a vision. And this vision, and the relentless pursuit of this vision, is grounded in something bigger than any individual.

The vision: To see all people, especially young people, who have been marginalized, oppressed and/or silenced, regain a sense of identity, belonging, and purpose that all people are deserving of. And for communities of marginalized, oppressed and silenced peoples, education has been the primary bridge used to escape poverty, racism, and to varying degrees, trauma.

A Culture of Competition or Cooperation?

To understand the issue, we have to first accept the following as truth: At any time, one of two cultures is prevalent—a culture of competition or a culture of cooperation. Now that this is established, we can proceed. When a culture of competition is prevalent, the systems within it cultivate and foster individualism and self gain. People strive to get ahead. Predator or prey. Those with the most privilege are the biggest and most powerful predators in the jungle of life; "biggest" and "most powerful" refer to the systems which are designed to allow these individuals to rise to the top tier. And all individuals are on these tiers. What separates the individuals at the top from the individuals at the bottom are the systems' oppressors. By definition, oppression is prolonged cruel or unjust treatment or control. So, when discussing the people at the lowest tiers, it's only right that we view them through the lens of oppressive treatments prescribed to the most marginalized. These treatments work harmoniously to oppress and exploit marginalized communities. These treatments are the microsystems that permeate our society. All are grounded in capitalism, an economic system attributed with private ownership and the acquisition of assets and capital. The individuals at the top are the ones who have the most investments, capital and assets.

When a culture of cooperation is prevalent, there's a sense of community, an understanding of cooperative work and shared economics. Individuals within this community who exemplify the best of this culture seek to abolish tiers that oppress, and instead choose to foster a sense of togetherness that organically creates empowerment and identity, empathy, and compassion. The most prevalent system is the absence of any tiers. Individuals creating space for outreach and shared resources that everyone is the recipient of.

This comes as a shock to no one that we live in a capitalist society. And in a capitalist society, as mentioned above, and as documented throughout history, time and time again, tiers and systems of oppression created and designed by the most privileged, strip entire peoples of their identity, community, and hope. They are always intended to remove the rungs on the ladder meant as supports to lift the most marginalized from the trenches of systemic poverty and inequity. As Baldwin says in *Nobody Knows My Name,* it is "extremely expensive" to be poor

(Baldwin, 1961). And the oppression felt and actualized by the most marginalized is illuminated in the struggles of our education system, which is a microcosm of society.

> Anyone who has ever struggled with poverty knows how extremely expensive it is to be poor.
>
> James Baldwin (1961)

The Impact of Inequitable Systems

Growing up in Chicago, living in the Robert Taylor projects, living in Section 8 housing, living in poverty and coming from the very communities mentioned above, I know firsthand the impact of inequitable systems. My mother had me when she was 16. By the time she was 25, she had five kids and later went on to have a sixth. My mother was a product of her environment and did everything in her power to make a better life for my four brothers and sister. When I was younger, my father was a huge part of my life. He wanted me to know what it meant to be a protector. He wanted me to know what it meant to be held accountable. He wanted me to know how to be tough…and many other things associated with both living to survive and misogyny.

As a kid, I found a lot of joy at school. I loved being there. And even though my family moved a lot, I remembered enjoying my teachers and my friends. Looking back, what made my educational experience so enjoyable, was that I had the fortune and privilege of being a good reader and student, who contributed in class (sometimes to a fault), participated in extracurricular activities, did well on all exams and state tests, and was able to culture switch between school and the neighborhood better than a lot of my peers. This distinction, admittedly very unfair, gave me opportunities a lot of my peers did not achieve in elementary school. For one, I was always affirmed by my teachers, publicly and privately. I remember the many times my teachers would share with me that I was "different" and "not like my friends." I remember receiving phone calls at home when my mom was told to "keep me on the right track" and how I had "so much potential." In fifth grade, I got to travel with my school's band to Disney World, where I got to perform and also participate in national band competitions. In sixth grade, I won the school spelling bee and was selected to represent our school at the Illinois state competition. "Thermos". "T-h-u-". Preceded by a "ding." It was my first word. I was so nervous.

In ninth grade, because of how well I performed on state tests, my high school advisory teacher enrolled me in pre-advanced and advanced placement (AP) courses for English and social studies. I was enrolled in general education classes for math and science, since I performed poorly on those tests and in those subject areas. I was fortunate that the teachers in my AP courses cultivated a culture of cooperation. This nurturing of a healthy classroom culture allowed me to experience quality instructional experiences. Friends helped me with things I struggled with academically and affirmed me in areas where I was strong. Teachers gave me quality feedback and empowered me to question the authors and ideas behind the literature and historical movements.

In elementary school, I wanted to be like my uncle. Uncle Puggy. He was my mom's little brother and the coolest guy on the South Side of Chicago. He was also my favorite babysitter. It was Valentine's Day and I was home with my uncle and his girlfriend. I remember walking to the kitchen to make a bowl of cereal. I remember walking back past my uncle's bedroom and seeing his girlfriend holding his gun and accidentally shooting him in the face. I dropped my cereal and rushed to his side. He died in my arms. I remember being sad. I remember my grandma and my aunts and my ma crying. I remember the trial and taking the stand to explain what I had seen. I remember the not guilty verdict. I remember my aunt playing Boyz II Men *End of the Road* on repeat and crying almost every day. Funny thing, I don't remember therapy. The normalization of past traumatic experiences are the direct result of living in systemic poverty which didn't and doesn't afford many, if any, safe spaces to heal.

My mother moved us from the East Side of Chicago to the North Side of Minneapolis at the start of my high school journey.

At the time, I hated her for it. She said she did it because she wanted us to have an opportunity to have a better life than she had. She was gang affiliated as a teenager. She sold drugs and hustled to provide for us. She wanted us to know a different way of surviving and providing. We moved into my granddad's one-bedroom apartment in north Minneapolis where he lived with the woman who stayed by his bedside until he passed from cancer in the spring of 2016. His living arrangements did not have the capacity to sustain my mother, my four brothers, my sister and me staying there, and within a month of his passing, we were staying at Mary's Place, a homeless shelter in north Minneapolis. Looking back, these were some of the best moments of my life. My family was together and we had so much hope. What more could you want?

It was in high school, and I would argue even middle school, where the ability to escape the realities of the community in school were no longer sustainable. My mother and I had a strained relationship. When I left for college, she didn't even know I left. But in school, socially, I was thriving due to my experiences in my AP courses. I attribute a lot of my early belief in myself academically to this experience because this is where I garnered hope. The opportunities afforded to me gave me exposure to experiences that my friends simply weren't getting—model United Nations, Youth in Government, free tickets to poetry slams, affirmations, resources, a road to hope. I got to experience and network with so many different people, all of whom had so many different life experiences. I was beginning to unlearn a stereotyped summation on who I had to be as a Black man in America, while simultaneously growing my sense of hope and purpose in the world because of everything I was privileged to experience during my middle and high school years. We must "learn to lift as we climb," as Angela Davis says (Davis, 1989). The beginning of learning and unlearning what it means to be a Black man in America, and applying the growth and the wisdom, and humility, and empathy, and compassion that comes with it has been, and will continue to be, lifelong work. And I would argue, the most worthy work I can do.

The process of empowerment cannot be simplistically defined in accordance with our own particular class interests. We must learn to lift as we climb.

Angela Davis (1989)

As many of you know, community colleges don't have dorms. You need to live in an apartment. My dad wanted to help me start college the right way, and so as a graduation gift, he gave me the gift of paying my rent for the first three months and my security deposit. The check bounced and neither me or the property manager could reach my dad. I needed to either come up with the money or move out. I went to the financial aid office and took out every loan possible. I knew for me, at that time in my life, moving home would entrench me back into the poverty that I fought so desperately to escape. When you are in the systems and inflicted with the systems' burdens, whether consciously or subconsciously, you normalize survival tactics grounded in escapism, and fighting and fleeing. I couldn't keep the tiny bit of hope that I had if I went back home. I stayed. And in doing so, sacrificed having money for groceries, sacrificed family, and being there for my brothers and sisters, to whom I was a father figure, for the betterment of myself, and my goals and dreams.

While in small-town rural Minnesota, something divine happened. Our basketball coach empathized with the culture shock that many of the Black and Brown students had in town. We were from all over the place: Chicago, Miami, Detroit, etc., all trying to make a name for ourselves. All trying to graduate with a two-year degree and move on to bigger and better things. In my coach's empathy, he worked with the community to assign us basketball families. I never grew close to my own basketball family, but one of my teammate's basketball family quickly became my own. My teammate's basketball family had a daughter who played on the women's basketball team. And after every home game, their family would invite all the players out to their farm for dinner. The mom, Kim, would debate with me all day long about dinner and supper. I could not fathom, this inner-city guy, how one could even *think* that dinner happened at *noon*. Growing up, dinner was whenever it happened, and that was usually after 9pm. It was never before 7pm and for damn sure, you didn't come home from school expecting dinner on the table. These debates brought me great joy, and Kim and I became close. I told her very early on that she was my mom and there just wasn't anything she could do about it. To my delight, she acquiesced.

One thing life in poverty teaches you is to depend solely on oneself. That's backwards, right? The most disadvantaged groups and people, who have very little, even within their families and communities, don't share or support or build up each other. For so long, I thought this was the result of the people. It took a lot of lived experiences and unlearning to recognize how different systemic barriers forced people from within fragile communities to normalize this culture of competition and separation, and self gain. This normalization, coupled with a strained relationship with my parents, had me seeking love, even when I didn't know I was seeking it or what I was seeking, or what love was. I didn't know how to love myself, or believe in myself. Therefore, I was not equipped with the agency necessary to grow my awareness, decision-making and discipline. I had one foot in the neighborhood and my old life, and one foot in the life I was trying to manifest for myself. As a result, I made bad choices, I wasn't responsible, was placed on academic probation *twice* and arrested for stupid things time and time again—traffic tickets, marijuana possession, and warrants for not showing up for court. Mind you, all the while "attending" school. And in spite of this, my mother, Kim, and her family chose to love on me unapologetically.

I was arrested the Friday of spring break of my freshman year in college. The two friends with me at the time posted bond and left town right away, no longer wanting to communicate with me, thinking that I would tell on them, which I never did. I was broke and alone, and thought that I would spend my entire spring break behind bars. But that Monday, I was bailed out. Guess who? Kim. I was relieved but felt an immense amount of shame. Although I had accomplished more than anyone in my family by simply graduating high school, and leaving home for college, I still wasn't actualizing my potential. This situation conveyed that more than any other, and at the time, not having much of an identity and sense of self-worth to stand on, I internalized my mistakes as my identity. I felt that every failure belonged to me, and every success or achievement was just more pressure to carry the torch and prove my worth to myself, my peers and to any- and everyone anywhere and everywhere. While walking out of the jailhouse, overly apologetic, Kim finally told me to shut up. She said, I would never have to pay her back, that I would pay it forward.

That following holiday break when everyone was going home, I had to stay in town because I couldn't afford to go home and my family didn't have much money. Of course, I didn't dare ask anyone to help me with this. How dare my ego have unlimited levels of audacity? Anyway, it was Christmas Eve. I was watching *Troy* in my room when I heard a voice from my window calling my name. I walked over to the window, and guess who? Kim. And her daughter, Katie. They told me that they wouldn't allow me to spend Christmas alone, and drove me out to their farm. While there, they gave me one of the greatest and most memorable gifts that I have ever received in my life—a blue and green reversible knitted blanket that they made themselves. This meant and still means so much to me because it was one of the first times that I remember receiving a gift just because. I didn't get care packages at college, I didn't even know what those were. So for somebody, who I felt didn't even know me deeply, to love on me and feel I was deserving of something so genuine, was powerful beyond words. I was not used to receiving gifts or things without conditions. I wasn't used to being seen in a positive light without doing or being something for someone. This was the beginning of me starting to accept that even if I don't believe in me, the way others sacrificed their time, and resources, and love for me, and affirmed me, I needed to rely on their perception of me more than I relied on my own perception.

I carried this grace with me to a four-year university, where I made the dean's list for the first time in my college career. The young man who barely graduated high school was on the dean's list. I felt I was making those around me proud. Equipped with this mindset of paying it forward, I decided to switch my major from political science to English and education. I wanted to pay it forward and I wanted to serve. More importantly, I wanted to serve in a community where the people who look like me and who endured a similar lived experience could have someone that did for them what so many people had done for me.

I graduated college, and did my student teaching experience living out of the trunk of a car that I had just bought as a graduation present to myself. My brother was shot and I was released from my experience because my cooperating teacher thought I wasn't recognizing how important my role was. There was no empathy to what I was living and the trauma my family and I were enduring. Not from him at least. My supervising teacher at my university, Dr. Karen Moroz, who also doubled and at times tripled, as my professor and mentor, embodied a lot of what I know for a fact I needed. As I caught the city bus to meet with Dr. Moroz, I resigned myself to the fact that I would be dropped from the program due to my inability to meet the duties outlined by my cooperating teacher. And this, I knew, would result in me being a failure, living paycheck to paycheck. I walked into her office and, after discussing the hurt I felt for my brother, the struggle I was having in prioritizing family over myself and my responsibilities, she did something I didn't see coming. Instead of dropping me from the program, she gave me $200 and a bus card. That was money to have groceries and gas to make it to my new student teaching experience and a bus card for days I didn't have cash. I felt so undeserving. Then, she proceeded to give me a new student teaching assignment. There was a principal at a school who knew me and was willing to give me a second chance. Apparently, the AP history teacher that I had in high school was now a principal. And he went from giving me opportunities to cultivating and nurturing my hope, to cultivating it even more. Talk about divine intervention.

I finished my student teaching, attained my teaching license, and chose to teach at a school in north Minneapolis. In my first year, I taught kindergarten, first grade, a specialist class, and ended the year in a seventh and eighth grade blended English language arts (ELA) class. I walked into the school, proud of coming from that community, arrogant and naive in my belief that since I came from that community, I knew everything about the young people in front of me. I walked into that school, into the profession of teaching, wholeheartedly believing that because of my own lived experience and my degrees, that I would teach those scholars more than they taught me. I couldn't have been more wrong.

Learning from Students

The irony in teaching is the overwhelming realization that *everything* required to be an effective educator is grounded in recognizing the importance of being a lifelong learner. In order to truly teach or inspire, I had to learn. And the students were teaching me every day. I learned how to tie a tie from my students, I learned how to show empathy from my students, how to grow my humility from my students, and how to empower the identity of my students by equipping them with cognitive skills that would transfer and translate to their confidence and growing sense of self-worth. Most importantly, my students taught me how to listen. The ability to listen and hear my students is where I needed to start. And the students who taught me these most crucial lessons weren't the ones who I would consider "easy." They were the ones who challenged me, unapologetically, with disregard for any title I had. Looking back, I couldn't be the educator I am without the constant attrition that comes when one begins to trade in ego for growing humility, empathy, and compassion.

Equity and Culturally Responsive Practices

And all of this leads us here, discussing one of the trendiest words in the last decade: equity. All across the country, speakers, facilitators, authors, educators, and community leaders are asking, "What does it mean to value equity?," "How do we create equity?," "What role does race play in equity?" "How can we create systems that foster equity?" And my answer, which I began to contextualize in the opening, harkens us to accept that systems do not create equity. People do.

We can't have the conversation about equity without first acknowledging that equitable actions and solutions are a byproduct of being a culturally responsive practitioner. And to be a culturally responsive practitioner, we have to accept our role as coconspirators in the abolishment of systems that deprive young people of the rungs needed to rise above the unjust treatments prescribed by the very systems from which we all are a part of. To be *truly* culturally responsive, which we all as educators and leaders should aspire to be, we have to own our role in staying grounded with a radical mindset shift that seeks to lift up and defend against injustice. And to truly fight against injustice, we have to know what we are fighting against. And what we are fighting against is not an individual. We are fighting against ideas. We are fighting against racism. We are fighting against misogyny. We are fighting against poverty. We are fighting against homophobia. We are fighting against xenophobia. And the most glaring truth is, none of those fights matter, until we mobilize as people and educators in the fight against capitalism, which is the creator of every other systemic form of oppression.

What I hope my life illustrates, and my experiences in the classroom convey, is this truth: Escaping microsystems will only get you but so far before you need people. We need an abolishment of a culture that has fostered, cultivated and nurtured a culture of competition and greed, and hatred since the founding of America. Capitalism, and its cronies (racism, and every other -ism or system that is grounded in oppression), seek to divide us, and seek to keep us ignorant and grounded in fear. These outcomes perpetually create generations of young people who are born into the school to prison pipeline simply by being born. The gaps are prevalent at birth because poverty is a byproduct of the system, not a creator of one. Make no mistake about it, the school to prison pipeline, the achievement gap or whatever you want to call it, starts at birth and ends at death, both literally and figuratively.

Well, what do we do with this newfound understanding of how systems connect, influence, and work together to oppress the hope of entire communities? How do we educate and lead with such a daunting reality at the forefront of the lived experiences of our students who we want to see thrive in the world? We fight. Together. Grounded in everything it means to be culturally responsive. Knowing that being culturally responsive is to be for the people.

As culturally responsive practitioners, we grow our agency by:

1. *Acknowledging the very systems on which every system stands or lives through: Capitalism.* Accepting that capitalism at the core of every single form of oppression is where we have to start in order to have the awareness of the culture we seek to destroy. The culture of competition that festers and permeates in our society wants us to stay divided and grounded in fear. It wants us to seek to compare, and to look for ways to make certain people "better" and others "worse." Accept this reality because in the acceptance of it comes an awareness necessary to transfer our empathy into compassion.

2. *Doing the work.* Behind every teacher's title is a human being. Each of us, with our own lived experience, shape how we show up in the world and in our classrooms. Recognizing the role that capitalism plays in our world helps us understand the varying degrees of privilege we have based on which tier we are on. For me, I have privilege. This was new to me. I had to recognize the privilege I have in being a man. Being a man affords me opportunity and safety that women simply do not have. I had to 100% humble myself and accept this truth. And in doing so, I am learning and unlearning what it means to be a man. This evolution in my perspective is growing my empathy which affords me the honor of becoming a better human, which makes me a better teacher and leader.

3. *Fostering, nurturing, and cultivating a radical culture of cooperation.* My life is the embodiment of how individual

people sacrificed their own self-interests for mine. Because the individuals who have impacted me were grounded in a sense of service, collectivism and cooperation, they didn't see me as less than or beneath them on a lower tier. They saw me as someone who lacked agency and capacity due to systems that were outside of my control. And in doing so, they sought to see me as someone deserving of the same quality of education, empowerment, and opportunity as them. I know and believe these individuals love and continue to love me as an equal. To be seen and loved and acknowledged for everything you are and everything you are not is one of the greatest forms of liberation. Give students quality classroom and instructional experiences that are grounded in the belief that *all* students are capable, regardless of where they come from, what they look like or how they act. Expose them to quality opportunities that afford them opportunities to grow their perspective. Affirm them. Give them grace. When one is given grace, one feels loved unconditionally. And when young people are loved unconditionally, they become infinite.

4. *Transferring empathy into compassion.* How I see it, empathy is the ability to feel and resonate with a person or group of people. I have no doubt that billions of people around the world empathize with those affected by injustice. Not many are willing to sacrifice their own self-interest for the betterment of people or ideas that don't directly benefit them as individuals. I had to recognize that even my own lived experience didn't allow me to have the level of empathy or compassion needed to be the servant I aspired to be. To better understand this concept, I want to quote a poem by William Cowper, entitled *Pity for Poor Africans*:

I own I am shock'd at the purchase of slaves,
And fear those who buy them and sell them are knaves;
What I hear of their hardships, their tortures, and groans

Is almost enough to draw pity from stones.
I pity them greatly, but I must be mum, For how could we
   do without sugar and rum?

William Cowper (1826)

Herein lies a man that empathized and thoroughly under-stood the hardship of the oppressed, but lacked the compassion to sacrifice for a greater good. This is where, by simply living in the system that we do, many people fall. Compassion isn't feeling for someone. Compassion isn't recognizing the struggles or hardships or sadness that one endures. It's to recognize *all* of that *and then* go out and actionably sacrifice and stand with the oppressed. To sacrifice whatever is necessary so that *all* people can truly be liberated and empowered.

Doing the Work

So I ask and answer my own question. What is equity? Equity is simply actionable hope. When people have hope, genuine hope, they not only recognize the vision and mission, which is to give *all* people an opportunity to have quality in all facets of their life, but to also *feel* a sense of belonging and connectedness to this mission. It is to see all people, especially young people, who have been marginalized, oppressed and/or silenced, regain a sense of identity, belonging, and purpose that all people deserve. I unapologetically demand that we ask ourselves, "How can I do the work necessary in order to be honorable, compassionate, and equitable in my actions?" And work steadfastly, together, hand in hand if need be, to abolish any and every system not created for all people to be equipped with hope. As Maya Angelou once said, "Hope and fear cannot occupy the same space. Invite one to stay" (Angelou, 2017). By the people and *always* unapologetically for the people.

Resources

Angelou, M. (2017). The Collected Autobiographies of Maya Angelou. New York, NY: The Modern Library.

Baldwin, J. (1961). Fifth Avenue, Uptown: a Letter from Harlem. In J. Baldwin (Ed.). *Nobody Knows My Name*. New York, NY: Dial Press.

Cowper, W. (1826). *The Negro's Complaint: A Poem. To which is added, Pity for Poor Africans*. London: Harvey and Darton.

Davis, A.Y. (1989). *Women, Culture, and Politics*. New York, NY: Vintage Books.

9

Getting the Right People on the Bus
Deepening Racial Consciousness in Hiring Practices to Support Racial Equity Transformation in Schools

Josh Seldess

Without question, when the majority of students in public schools are students of color and only 18 percent of our teachers are teachers of color, we have an urgent need to act. We've got to understand that all students benefit from teacher diversity. We have strong evidence that students of color benefit from having teachers and leaders who look like them as role models and also benefit from the classroom dynamics that diversity creates. But it is also important for our white students to see teachers of color in leadership roles in their classrooms and communities.

The question for the nation is how do we address this quickly and thoughtfully?

Education Secretary John B. King Jr.,
speaking at Howard University, March 8, 2016.
(US Department of Education; Office of Planning,
Evaluation and Policy Development; Policy and
Program Studies Service, 2016)

Educators across the United States have never accurately reflected the racial demographics of the students we teach. In 2016, the US Department of Education released a report entitled, *The State of Racial Diversity in the Educator Workforce*, which included research findings that showed teachers of color are more likely to have higher expectations of students of color (as measured by higher numbers of referrals to gifted programs); confront issues of racism; serve as advocates and cultural brokers; and develop more trusting relationships with students, particularly those with whom they share a cultural background. (US Department of Education; Office of Planning, Evaluation and Policy Development; Policy and Program Studies Service, 2016) Nevertheless, an analysis conducted in 2019 by *The Washington Post* of school district data from 46 states and the District of Columbia found that only one tenth of 1% of Latinx students attended a school system where the relative proportion of Latinx teachers equaled or exceeded the proportion of Latinx students. Black students fared only slightly better in this study: 7% were enrolled in a district where the share of Black teachers matched or exceeded that for students. Among Asian students, it was 4.5%. Meanwhile, 99.7% of White students attended a district where the faculty was as White as the student body (Meckler & Rabinowitz, 2019). Schools in the United States have clearly failed to racially diversify the workforce, especially among teachers and administration. Not entirely coincidentally, schools in the United States have simultaneously failed to eliminate the racial predictability of which students occupy the highest and lowest academic achievement groups, which students are the least and most likely to be excluded from classroom instruction due to disciplinary action, and which students are least and most likely to be referred to special education by race. As has been well documented by parents, students, educators, researchers, and activists alike, the United States has a persistent race problem that runs through our culture and institutions, and there is no place where it is more insidious than in education.

Education, like other social institutions in the United States, has historically served to uphold White supremacy. Both educator workforce demographics and student outcomes persistently reflect the racial hierarchy upon which this country was built.

In many instances, this happens in the absence of conscious racial prejudice and despite the best intentions of classroom teachers and school administration. Instead, schools tend to normalize White supremacy by centering White cultural characteristics in every facet of schooling, from what it means to "learn," to what it means to "teach," to what it means to "behave," to what it means to "know." Because White supremacy is tightly woven into the fabric of the larger society, it readily becomes synonymous with "normality" and, as such, its presence and positionality in schools goes largely unexamined, even as we who work in the field, and in much of society, continue to lament the racial inequities that permeate education. In US schools, implicit biases favoring White cultural norms routinely become self-fulfilling prophecies, which, consciously or unconsciously, institutionalize White supremacy throughout entire educational systems and perpetuate racial disparities in student outcomes and hiring practices alike.

As a White teacher and administrator at the high school and middle school levels for over 20 years, I have come to believe strongly that White supremacy and systemic racism erode the potential of schools to responsibly educate *all* students, most particularly students of color and especially Black males. Interrupting institutionalized racism in schools requires a systemic approach involving a careful examination of how classroom curriculum, instructional practices, professional development, student and faculty support, and community relations operate to either challenge or uphold the racial status quo. It is also critical to consider how the racial demographics of the adults working within our schools and school districts either promote or inhibit the institution's capacity for change. Like other social institutions in a White supremacist society, schools have historically been positioned to meet the needs of the dominant racial group. Thus, when a vast majority of educators within a school are White, or comprise the groups holding the bulk of institutional power, a real danger exists that we will struggle to recognize the *systemic* barriers to academic success facing Black and Brown students, rigidly yet erroneously attributing any struggles they may have to deficits in the students themselves and their families rather than to the machinations of White supremacy that educational foundations were built on. It is important to note that all students face challenges in school—or at least, on some level, they should. Challenge is part of a rigorous educational experience when applied mindfully and with consideration to the unique learning needs of individual students. Furthermore, all students may face challenges outside of school that present very real obstacles to success, including individual and family concerns related to health, emotional well-being, tragedy, and loss that impact their ability to fully access the learning opportunities in the classroom. Only students of color, however, face the institutional obstacles to success created by attending schools steeped in systemic racism and White supremacy *in addition to* obstacles that are faced more universally which can and do impact individual White students and families as well. It can be difficult for White administrators and teachers to comprehend the cultural adaptations needed to educate all students because, by and large, schools have historically worked for us within the context of White supremacy—or, at the very least, they were designed to. Multiple racial perspectives are needed at all levels in education in order to counter the racial misconception of many White educators that well-intentioned schools have transcended institutionalized racism simply because they are well-intentioned, and in spite of racially disaggregated data that suggests otherwise. Incorporating the voices of students and community members of color in all decision-making will go a long way towards a critical understanding of racism in schools. Nevertheless, any comprehensive systemic racial equity trans-formation plan must consider how the racial demographics of various roles in the building, and the corresponding racial consciousness of these adults working directly with students, impact school culture, educational practices, and ultimately stu-dent outcomes.

Growing Up White

Growing up as a White male student attending public schools in suburban Chicago, I clearly benefitted from having teachers who genuinely appeared to take an interest in me, assumed that I had worth as a person, encouraged me to take academic and extracurricular risks (which I was generally not inclined to do), and set challenging expectations that forced me to grow. The fact that most of my teachers were also White (but not all—a fact I will return to) was unremarkable to me—a racial context that seemed *normal* and to which I gave little to no conscious thought. Having teachers and school leaders who looked like me helped establish a cultural and psychological congruence in school that I took for granted, yet which undeniably contributed to a sense of belonging and helped assure my academic success. Seeing myself reflected racially in most of my teachers and within the dominant cultural norms of my schools was an invisible advan-tage I was afforded that, statistically speaking, many students of color could not claim then, and still do not share. Combine my racial, yet largely unconscious, experiences in school with the relentless exposure to normalized images and representations of White supremacy pervasive in US culture at large, and it was predictable that I would come to see myself as capable and deserving of success, which aided me not just in my elementary and secondary classrooms, but which also propelled me through my experiences in higher education and have carried over later throughout life. This often plays out for me in strongly held, yet often unconsciously, beliefs that schools are operating largely as they should because they have typically worked well for me—as they have historically worked well for White people as a demographic. As an educator, these beliefs often play out as implicit biases favoring Whiteness which, both wittingly and unwittingly, safeguard and perpetuate White cultural norms.

Although I was a student who grew up benefitting from access to educators who looked like me, I was also a student who benefitted from access to educators who did not. I attended public schools in a community that prided itself on its racial diversity, which I believe accounted for this privilege. For example, the principal of the elementary school I attended was Black, as were both building administrators at the middle school I walked to every day. Thus, even as I was being subtly indoctrinated into the norms of White culture through schooling and the larger society, it was also normal for me to come to school and see Black and Brown people in esteemed roles and positions of authority. This was important because it helped paint a more accurate portrait of race and promoted a healthier racial psyche by interrupting the White supremacist narrative that only White people possess the qualities and qualifications to be in charge.

Furthermore, when compared to my White teachers, I distinctly recall the different ways my teachers of color managed their classrooms and challenged dominant cultural assumptions about learning and knowing, even though I would never have thought of it this way at the time. One of my Black middle school teachers judiciously taught our social studies class through a racial counter-narrative, imbedding the perspectives of people of color and other marginalized groups into the teaching of US history before it was ever in vogue. Perhaps in none of my other classes at that time could a racially or culturally diverse group of students potentially "see themselves" reflected in the curriculum of their US history class, and when they did, it would likely be through the distorted lens of the dominant culture. I can honestly say that, for me, it was in this class, with this Black male social studies teacher, where I was first taught to interrogate the idea of a monolithic "truth" (indeed, where I first learned that was even possible) and to think critically about the world around me in ways that some White people may never be expected to do. It's not the case that my White teachers couldn't have also potentially taught their classes this way; it's that they didn't—a fact reflecting, among other things, the respective racial consciousness of the teachers.

I also recall having an English language arts class (ELA) in middle school with a bilingual, Spanish-speaking Latina teacher who periodically (albeit ironically) gave directions or partial explanations to the entire class in Spanish. Looking back, I believe she did this primarily so the handful of her Spanish-speaking students could see and hear their own culture reflected back to them linguistically in the classroom—something I suspect otherwise did not happen. Nevertheless, as a White student, this was perhaps the most memorable and influential ELA class I ever had. Similar to other monolingual students, I could not easily understand what my teacher was saying in Spanish (a valuable lesson in culture and empathy, in and of itself). Ms. Silva taught us to rely upon key vocabulary (which was very limited in my case), context clues, and other literacy strategies to construct meaning from what she said, which were the same literary strategies she taught us to use when grappling with any challenging text. Fortunately for me, we were also allowed to seek assistance from our Spanish-speaking peers as needed, positioning my bilingual classmates as the most resourced students in the room and interrupting the dominant cultural norm that English is the only legitimate language used for instruction in school. Furthermore, these occasions clearly illustrated to me why speaking multiple languages was a cultural *asset* that my bilingual classmates brought into the classroom, rather than any sort of deficit as speaking Spanish is sometimes portrayed to be in a White supremacist society. Ms. Silva always framed rigorous literacy instruction in the form of a riddle or challenging problem to be solved, in any language—a way of deciphering a code to reveal the sometimes hidden meaning of a text, which made me enjoy the challenge of reading and helped me learn a little bit of Spanish along the way.

It is in no way a coincidence that these effective instructional strategies were approaches my teachers of color utilized in the classroom, but my White teachers did not. This is primarily because most White teachers lack the will, skill, knowledge, and/or capacity to do so—and perhaps all of the above. Furthermore, the benefits to me as a White student growing up with the privilege of having outstanding educators of color is not the most compelling reason to insist upon racial diversity at every level of schools. As a White student, it was an invisible advantage to have a majority of teachers who looked like me; yet I also derived clear benefit from having teachers who did not. This is a hallmark of systemic racism in that the system works to serve the interests of students in the dominant racial group— either way. Importantly, based on student outcomes in most schools, this is not the way the system works for many students of color; and for the many students of color who do excel, it is often in spite of the system rather than an outcome of schooling in the United States that they can readily rely on. Researchers have found that Black and Brown students who have teachers who match their race or ethnicity experience better attendance, fewer suspensions, more positive attitudes, higher test scores, higher graduation rates, and higher college attendance than those who do not (Meckler & Rabinowitz, 2019). There are obviously many variables impacting student achievement other than the racial dynamics between teachers and students in schools. Nevertheless, in a moment in history when talk of racial equity and the elimination of racial achievement disparities proliferates throughout the field of education, it is important to examine the racial backdrop in which student achievement historically and predictably does or does not occur.

Getting the Right People on the Bus

Given that what is at stake is our schools' capacity to provide all students with an equitable education, regardless of race, schools have a moral obligation to hire and retain a racially diverse workforce. Hiring for racial equity begins with the work of human resources (HR), and recruiting a robust pool of qualified and diverse applicants. I have never worked in HR nor do I claim to have knowledge or insights to share from that lens. What I do have to share is over 20 years of experience as a teacher and administrator chairing or serving on countless hiring committees, as well as my observations about effective hiring practices from a racial equity lens. From this perspective, I offer five key concepts towards deepening racial consciousness around your school's hiring practices that support the broader work of systemic racial equity transformation in schools.

1. Conduct a Hiring Needs Assessment from a Racial Equity Lens

Every district I have worked for has espoused the belief in hiring a racially diverse workforce. Nevertheless, when hiring is concluded, the results often reflect the racial status quo, making racially diverse hiring seem more like a liberal-minded intention than an actual priority in practice. Many building and department-level hiring assessments begin and end by identifying the needs of the organization rather than the needs of the students they serve. Often, hiring needs are determined by citing the individuals who will not be returning and listing the roles and related job descriptions that need to be filled for the upcoming school year. This begins the process discussed later of identifying candidates with the experience, skills, and credentials to fill those vacancies, and conducting a process to hire the best one.

By first assessing student achievement data and other relevant information, however, and then disaggregating that data by race, it is possible to gain a deeper understanding of the needs of your organization related to racial equity. Compare the racial demographics of your students to information showing which students are meeting or exceeding academic benchmarks. Make the same comparisons using disciplinary data as well. If data disproportionately shows White students near the top or students of color disproportionately near the bottom as it does in many schools (or the reverse trends when looking at disciplinary data), it is likely that systemic racism is playing a significant role. Then examine the demographics of the various roles in your school or department and determine whether all students, or just some, have access to teachers who look like them in the classroom and role models who look like them in all aspects of the school who then can readily emulate for success. Finally, assess the racial composition of the committees and decision-making bodies in your organization and consider which racial perspectives may be missing and how those missing perspectives might inhibit the racial equity goals of your organization. When this level of assessment reveals institutional inequity, then systemic steps must be taken, including intentionally and unapologetically hiring "qualified" candidates of color over other "qualified" candidates whenever possible in the service of racially equitable outcomes for students.

2. Interrogate Cultural Norms and Institutional Racial Bias

Most organizations are only vaguely aware of the dominant cultural norms that exist and perpetuate those norms during the hiring process. Entire institutions, hiring committees, and the individuals that comprise them both, often start with conscious or unconscious beliefs about who will be a "good fit" to work in their school. A candidate may be perceived as a "good fit" when they come to an organization with a set of cultural characteristics that closely align with the organizational culture that already exists. Many of us have heard or used the phrase, *it's not what you know, but who you know, that gets you a job in education*. This common saying reflects the bias shown towards considering those who are familiar to us or share common connections as the "best fit" or most reliable sources of incoming talent. This form of bias can help safeguard or reinforce some of the traditions or perceived strengths of a school. However, when a defining characteristic of familiarity is *race*, because most of our society continues to be highly racially segregated, this constitutes a form of racial bias that consciously or unconsciously perpetuates existing deficits in the racial experiences and perspectives of educators that are needed to successfully educate *all* students. In other words, from the framework of the dominant culture, hiring those we know or who seem most like "us" is a highly effective way to maintain the racial status quo; and when it comes to achieving goals related to racial equity, this is something that most schools cannot afford to do. HR can help by conducting audits to check for patterns in previous work experience, education, and personal job references, in addition to the race of the candidates hired in each role over the past ten years to help assess the level of this form of racial bias in your school's hiring practices, and to provide one indication of whether your school is building the capacity to achieve its racial equity goals.

I have heard many well-intentioned educators lament that their efforts to increase the hiring percentages of racially diverse educators is thwarted by a lack of qualified applicants of color in the candidate pool. To be sure, HR departments need to solidify their recruiting practices to assure a depth of qualified candidates of all races, but most particularly qualified candidates of color. That being said, however, it is important to root out racial biases that may be eliminating qualified candidates of color from consideration who are already there! Hiring processes begin by combing through the resumes, cover letters, and other paperwork submitted by candidates aspiring to interview for a position in your school. When identifying the characteristics of a highly desirable candidate, the preference of certain criteria over others may reveal implicit racial bias as well.

A colleague recently shared a poignant example of how this form of bias finds its way into the hiring process, despite best intentions. It is important to note that this colleague is a White male, like myself, who also has many years of training in racial equity leadership and approaches the hiring process from a racial equity lens. When vetting his initial stack of applications, he typically looks for certain features to separate a smaller number of candidates to schedule for an interview. Hiring from a racial equity lens means intentionally looking for indicators that a qualified candidate is likely a person of color, such as honors, group affiliations, or a degree from an historically Black college or university (HBCU), and positioning that individual in the group of prospective interviewees. Noting in one situation that a well-qualified applicant included in her resume an affiliation with a Black sorority while attending a local college, he added her name to the list of candidates to move to the interview phase of the process. At the end, realizing that he had the luxury of interviewing more candidates than his committee had time set aside for, he started to pare his list down even further until the last interview slot came down to a decision between the applications of two qualified candidates, neither of whom had prior teaching experience. One candidate's application materials were racially neutral and included a degree in education from a highly prestigious university, and the other candidate's application showed her affiliation with a Black sorority while attending a local college. My colleague described to me how quickly prioritizing racial equity fell to the wayside due to the allure of potentially hiring a candidate with the esteemed academic credentials of the former. He later recognized the conditioning of White dominant cultural norms led him to overvalue the status brought by esteemed academic credentials, regardless of whether that individual also carried the potential to most effectively educate all students. Furthermore, he acknowledged in hindsight that an allure to hiring a candidate with these credentials over someone who attended college locally was imagining the praise he would likely receive from his peers for successfully recruiting a young teacher with this "pedigree" into the organization.

Acknowledging White racial bias is the first step towards interrupting it. Having done so, he realized he would need to modify the parameters he had created in order to adhere to his commitment to racial equity. He could either choose to interview the candidate he felt sure was a person of color instead of the other candidate in spite of their academic credentials, or he could create an additional interview spot in order to have the opportunity to interview them both. Doing neither, however, would perpetuate the misperception that there were fewer qualified candidates of color in the applicant pool than there actually were. Interviews and further vetting ultimately reveal more about the best candidate for any position, but it is clear that no candidate has the opportunity to be hired who is not even granted an interview. I was humbled by my colleague's willingness to share this story with me because it reflects a level of racial consciousness and ability to take ownership of one's own racial bias that White people in general, and White men in particular, don't often possess.

In light of the fact that much racial bias is implicit and operates at an unconscious level, HR departments can play a role in helping sustain a commitment to racial equity as well. For example, district-level administrators in a neighboring high school district helped assure that qualified candidates of color got interviews by requiring that all prospective new hires sent forward to HR must be selected from an interview pool comprised of no less than 50% candidates of color. In doing so, they guaranteed that hiring committees would speak directly to candidates of color as part of their hiring process, thus repositioning racial equity as a priority over other interview criteria that tend to reproduce the racial status quo in the workforce.

3. Establish a Racial Equity Hiring Committee

Most schools utilize hiring committees to interview candidates and determine which ones are best suited to work with the students in your school. A well balanced hiring committee begins by mindfully including representation from multiple perspectives. Consider individuals occupying roles other than classroom teachers to include on your committee. Support staff, including office assistants and paraprofessionals, often have a unique perspective on the needs of students, as well as the personal characteristics that lead to the greatest success in the classroom. Including one or more students on the committee brings a student perspective as well. Consider selecting students who have been academically "successful," as well as students who have not. Finally, including a parent on your hiring committee is an effective way to incorporate a valuable community perspective as well. Establishing a racial equity hiring committee means taking all these steps while also connecting your institutional equity goals to the process of selecting the right educators to achieve them. A racial equity hiring committee must include diverse racial perspectives among the individuals on the committee in an intentional effort to counter the sorts of conscious or unconscious racial bias described earlier.

In order for a racial equity hiring committee to effectively serve its purpose, the work must begin before interviewing the first candidate. Hold at least one meeting prior to interviews to engage members in courageous conversations about race, including making a collective commitment to holding one another mutually accountable for prioritizing racial equity in the hiring process. Most importantly, establish norms that give committee members equal voice in the vetting process and provide guidelines for navigating difficult racial conversations when they are needed. Honest discussions about race are often avoided in interracial spaces, primarily because they can elicit intense emotions, so it is vital that members of your racial equity hiring committee have the skill and tools at their disposal that will sustain healthy and productive conversations about race in the context of the hiring process.

We were wrapping up an interview process in a district that had incorporated these steps into their process when a member of our committee made the observation that, with regard to our post-interview discussions, the darker the skin of the candidates we interviewed, the more controversial the prospect of hiring that candidate became. It was an astute and accurate observation, and a courageous dynamic to name. Mustering the courage and commitment to name it, however, resulted in an honest and in-depth discussion about race among all members of the committee regarding the role race played in the vetting process for each of us. A Black parent on the committee acknowledged that she had been more critical of the candidates of color out of an unconscious wish to protect them. She explained her truth, that Black teachers would face harsher scrutiny in the workplace than their White counterparts, and she feared that Black teachers needed to be nearly impeccable to counter the unfair scrutiny they would receive. This was done from a protective instinct, and yet it also created additional hiring barriers for candidates of color. These conversations may be uncomfortable for members of the committee, but they are necessary. In this case, refusing to turn away from a courageous conversation about the powerful impact race was playing in our hiring process enabled our committee to better fulfill our commitment to racial equity.

4. Ask the Right Questions

While the hiring component of systemic racial equity transformation is best achieved by hiring candidates of color when given the opportunity to do so, it is also important not to rely on racial identity alone. The most important characteristic when hiring for racial equity is an awareness of the presence of race and mindfulness around the impact it has on teaching and learning. While people of color are far more likely to possess a sharper racial lens than White people due to the awareness that is needed to navigate a White supremacist society, it is a generalization and possibly quite problematic to assume that is always the case. Regardless of race, there are countless variables that shape an individual's racial consciousness, and it is possible for White people to develop a keen awareness of race as well. When interviewing candidates, it is important to ask questions that establish whether a candidate has had experiences that allow them to consider how their own race, as well as the race of their students, can impact the dynamics around teaching and learning. Here are examples of interview questions your racial equity hiring committee can ask that will help determine the racial consciousness of your candidates:

- ◆ Describe a culturally responsive lesson you have taught and how you knew whether it was effective.
- ◆ What would you do to raise the reading proficiency of your Black and Brown students? How will you know whether you were successful?
- ◆ What specific strategies would you incorporate to increase the participation of students of color in the orchestra program?
- ◆ What do you think is important for White students to know about their own racial identities?
- ◆ Explain what you would do to center your instruction around the lived experiences of all students you teach.
- ◆ Describe a culturally inclusive classroom. What would you do to make your classroom environment culturally and racially inclusive?
- ◆ Discuss any experiences you have had that helped you understand how your own racial identity, as well as the racial identities of your students, impacts the dynamics around teaching and learning.

Some candidates can speak from their own racial experiences and will be able to readily offer these as windows into how race might play out in the classroom. Others will struggle to name their own racial experiences, yet, on some level, recognize that racism plays out in schools as it does elsewhere, and these candidates may reveal an openness to better understanding how these dynamics operate in the classroom. Some candidates will reveal a rigid mindset with regard to the impact of race characterized by a belief they are "color-blind" and don't see race, or exhibit some form of deficit thinking regarding students of color. Candidates in this last category should be highly suspect if your goal is racial equity, and a racial equity hiring committee should be prepared to protect against bringing these educators into the organization where they may inadvertently inflict damage upon students of color (very few educators I have met do this on purpose), and in doing so, inflict damage upon White students who see this version of racism being validated in school as well. Candidates in the middle group, however, may be well positioned to help schools attain their racial equity goals. One such candidate, a White female just finishing her first year in the classroom, responded to the racial equity questions in her interview with something close to the following: "Those are really great questions, and to be honest, I have never thought about race in those ways before. I'm really glad you asked me those questions because they made me think about how important it is for me to learn more. Do you have any recommendations for how I can get started?" The committee unanimously recommended her to be hired.

5. Retain the Talent You Hire

To be sure, racial diversity is not the same as racial equity. Just as a culturally inclusive classroom environment is essential for students of color to thrive, so too is a culturally inclusive work environment essential for colleagues of color to prosper in the schools in which they work. Many of our colleagues of color grow weary from having to leave parts of themselves at the door in order to navigate the norms of the dominant culture that permeate most schools. If schools are unable to establish and sustain a racially equitable work environment, many of our colleagues of color may choose to leave and work elsewhere, rendering the work of any racial equity hiring practices ineffective. Make sure there is a way to gauge the experience of all educators in the workplace, and the particular needs of colleagues of color. Allocate time and resources to do whatever is needed to maintain a racially equitable work environment by listening carefully to what our colleagues of color have to say about the impact of race and racism in our schools.

Conclusion

"Equity" has become the new buzzword in education. The shift from *equality*, giving every student a fair share, to *equity*, giving every student what she or he needs in order to thrive, is an urgent moral imperative currently facing our schools. In a country built very literally upon institutionalized racism, and as steeped in White supremacy as ours, discussions of equity in education absent a deep commitment to *racially equitable outcomes* for students ring hollow and insincere. Our students and families of color are not broken. What is broken is the system that has been charged with serving them. Making sure we have racially conscious educators, and effective processes for hiring them, is one small, but important, step towards institutional racial equity transformation.

Resources

Meckler, L. and Rabinowitz, K. (2019, December 27). America's Schools are More Diverse than Ever. But the Teachers are still mostly White. *The Washington Post*. Retrieved from www.washingtonpost.com/graphics/2019/local/education/teacher-diversity.

US Department of Education; Office of Planning, Evaluation and Policy Development; Policy and Program Studies Service. (2016). *The State of Racial Diversity in the Educator Workforce*. Washington, D.C.

10

Being more than "The Help"

Marlena Gross-Taylor

My maternal grandmother was a housekeeper...for White people. She was "the help"—cleaning White peoples' houses and taking care of their children from 9:00 a.m. to 3:00 p.m. each weekday. Her father was a sharecropper until he finally "had enough," paid "the man" off "at all cost," got his wife and "bitsy babies," which included my grandmother, and walked up the railroad tracks to Denham Springs, Louisiana, to *freedom.*

Neither my grandmother nor her father were allowed a full education simply because they were Black and lived in southern Louisiana where Jim Crow laws severely limited their opportunities for both a comprehensive education and gainful employment. My grandmother and her father followed one of the few paths available to Black Americans in the early 1900s, which by law tied this once enslaved group of Americans to second-class citizenship, including low-paying sharecropping and domestic work. While I hold an incredible amount of pride in my grandmother and great-grandfather's journeys, their experiences are shared by nearly every Black American born here in the United States, particularly in the south.

Together, my grandmother and her husband were successful in spite of the limitations imposed on them by society; furthermore, they had a clear vision and plan for their children and grandchildren to elevate above the occupational hierarchy Black

Americans continue to be circumscribed in our country. Both my maternal and paternal grandparents were convinced that a good education paired with the knowledge (aka the ability to code-switch) to navigate the "White man's world" would all but ensure my destiny to rise above the occupational hierarchy. Not to sound cliché, but failure truly has not been an option in my family. Excellence was and is our family standard, as modeled by my parents and their siblings.

Even before I was of age to have a job as a teenager, I knew there were certain positions I would never be allowed to work. Both my grandmothers were adamant that I never work in any type of domestic role. In fact, my parents went a step further and did not permit my older brothers or me to work in the fast-food/restaurant industry either. School was our "job" and excelling academically was the minimum expectation. Being involved in the arts was also a requirement by my parents; this was a requirement in order to play sports to help further debunk stereotypes of Black athletes, and help ensure my brothers and I were well-rounded. If we were able to carve out time for a job, it had to be in an office setting so we could learn the culture and skills of business.

Trying to live up to my family's standard of excellence while juggling the exhaustion of being Black in America, navigating a society created to reinforce inferiority of Black and Brown people was and continues to be difficult at times. I take solace that I heeded the warnings and teachings of my parents and grandparents. In fact, I give them all full credit for my success today. My work ethic, diplomacy, code-switching, and intrinsic desire for growth were all learned from them. Moreover, I raised my children with the same lessons I was taught by my family, specifically around code-switching, often viewing this practice as a means to a greater end: Equality and equity in both career pathways and other opportunities in life.

Success is the ultimate form of resistance to systemic racism and inequities in our schools and communities; however, my advocacy continues to revolve around identifying the support necessary for our Black and Brown students in particular to be more than "the help" once they are adults and actually have unlimited opportunities to be successful and create a legacy of excellence. In order to eradicate the barriers Black Americans have had to endure, specifically around occupational hierarchy, we have to start with a systemic approach to increase stakeholder commitment to racial equity, coupled with intentional actions that truly value and support a culture rooted in equity and diversity.

There are three critical pillars to begin the work of eradicating occupational barriers for our students:

Awareness.
Action.
Reflection.

Awareness

One of my favorite quotes by Maya Angelou encourages us to "do better" in our actions and disposition once we "know better" after being properly informed on a given topic or idea. But what if you don't know what you don't know? How is it possible to "do better" when you do not "know better"? (Angelou, n.d.)

Before we, as educators, can initiate proper vision casting and skill building in schools of both our Black and Brown students, as well as the educators who support them, it is imperative we pause to audit our own racial knowledge and implicit bias.

Owning Our Bias

Confronting our unconscious bias is the catalyst for reframing our understanding of the impact stereotypes have had on our perception of racism and diversity. Let's face it, 2020 was traumatic not only due to a worldwide pandemic, but the polarizing political rhetoric targeted at diminishing what many Black Americans viewed as a second civil rights movement following the horrific death of George Floyd while in police custody. Add to those events a contentious presidential election that not only resulted in an historic election of our first female and Black Vice President, but also exposed a country divided by racial unrest.

There are several avenues to assess one's implicit bias; however I have found the most powerful starting point is to simply answer this question: Who do you spend your Saturdays with? In other words, when you have some free time not associated with work or family, are the people you spend that time with from a different race or ethnic background than your own? Increasing the diversity of your personal relationships not only expands your perspective but may also deepen your understanding and empathy for the lived experiences of marginalized populations. Proximity is the greatest factor of the lack of diverse relationships outside a work environment. It is human nature to seek out and associate with people who are similar to us in religious, political, economic, and racial terms; consequently, this tendency affects the lens through which we view the world, from the political polarization of society, to income inequality, and to racial differences in our friendships and personal relationships.

According to the Public Religion Research Institute (Piacenza, 2014), three quarters of White Americans have "entirely White social networks without any minority presence" (Piacenza, 2014). So, naturally, when the topic of racism is presented, White Americans are simply not socially positioned to truly understand the Black experience because they have not experienced it nor do they have diverse enough friendships to gain perspective before developing an opinion.

The Implicit Bias Test

Categorization is a fundamental quality of the human brain. We teach children, as early as infancy, how to sort and recognize differences in shapes, sounds, and letters until the process is automatic. The ability to quickly characterize people based on physical and social characteristics is part of our survival instinct but also the foundation of stereotypes which may lead to discriminatory beliefs and behavior.

Psychologists at Harvard University, the University of Virginia, and the University of Washington created "Project Implicit" (Project Implicit, n.d.) to measure unconscious or automatic biases via an implicit bias test. This test is free and publicly available. Cognitive shortcuts may lead to stereotyping, microaggressions, and subsequently biased behavior. Becoming aware of our biases can help reroute both our own and our students' cognitive shortcuts. Harvard research further suggests interventions, such as diversity training, elicit fairly immediate positive change in a person's implicit bias; however, the intervention must be ongoing until the change becomes automatic.

Learning and Teaching Truth

Having a clear understanding of the racist history of our country and how it plays out today in the form of racial trauma, implicit bias, and microaggression that Black and Brown students, their families, and even school employees experience, changes how districts interact and support the lived experiences of diverse individuals. Systemic racism in America simply cannot be an historical footnote taught superficially to protect the fragility of White students, White educators, and White families. So how do we begin to audit our historical knowledge gaps as educators, as well as the opportunity gaps of our students? Let's start with filling in the historical gaps we have as educators.

Discovering the Truth

As a history teacher, I shared with my students Winston Churchill's belief of history being written by the victor. Bestselling author, Dan Brown, explains this idea further:

> When two cultures clash, the loser is obliterated, and the winner writes the history books—books which glorify their own cause and disparage the conquered foe. As Napoleon once said, 'What is history, but a fable agreed upon?
>
> Dan Brown (2003)

The real question that we, as Americans first and educators second, must answer is who wrote the US history that we teach our students in school? Furthermore, does it include the whole truth and nothing but the truth?

After the Black Lives Matter protests from the summer of 2020, former President Trump deepened the racial division crippling the country by characterizing the racial injustice demonstrations as "left-wing rioting and mayhem" that "are the direct result of decades of left-wing indoctrination in our schools (Balingit & Meckler, 2020). Trump targeted Pulitzer prize winner The 1619 Project (www.nytimes.com/ interactive/2019/08/14/magazine/1619-america-slavery. html), which aims to reframe the country's history by placing the consequences of slavery and the contributions of Black Americans at the very center of our national narrative, and Trump wrongly asserts that the United States was founded on principles of "oppression, not freedom." Instead, Trump promised his administration would create a "pro-American history" to be taught in schools.

The current American history curriculum taught in schools is already pro-American, intentionally glossing over the ugly truth of our forefathers, who were slave owners, forging to create a new government based on freedom while codifying chattel slavery and anti-Blackness. The economic prosperity of the current United States was literally built upon the backs of enslaved Africans and generations of their descendants. While it may be tempting to believe not talking about systemic racism in our country is the solution to ending racism, that is simply not true. There are hundreds of years of history that all Americans need to know in order to first understand how racism continues to marginalize Black Americans and reinforce occupational hierarchy.

It is imperative that educators explore how to communicate and model productive engagement of critical race conversations for students. As a Black American with a mother who was a teacher and principal, studying Black history and learning about the specific experiences of my ancestors has been part of my family's standard of excellence. Noted below are three of my favorite resources to begin your journey of learning *all* of our country's history. I would encourage you to explore all three of these resources in the order presented to build your stamina, no matter your race or ethnicity, of being comfortable with being uncomfortable. Please note, this is by no means an exhaustive list of research-based resources, but I am convinced that these selections will ignite your journey of growth while informing your action steps to break the occupational hierarchy imposed on our Black and Brown students:

1. Talking About Race, The Smithsonian's National Museum of African American History & Culture provides tools and primary resources for educators, parents and equity allies to empower and engage in meaningful conversations and actions.

2. *White Fragility: Why it's so Hard for White People to Talk about Racism* by Robin DiAngelo examines the counterproductive reactions White people have when their assumptions about race are challenged, and how these reactions maintain racial inequality. Also includes a free reader's guide intended to support formal and informal discussions of White fragility.

3. *Caste: The Origins of Our Discontents* by Isabel Wilkerson explores the unrecognized hierarchy in America, its history and its consequences, which impact American culture today, a culture still defined by a hierarchy of human divisions. It is a part of Oprah's Book Club and podcast series, in which the book is discussed by the author and a diverse panel of book club participants.

Instructional Truth

As we learn and fortify our cultural knowledge gaps in American history, we must also analyze the very curriculum presented to students each day in all classes, not just history class. As Bill Russell says Black students must see themselves portrayed accurately in their curriculum resources to not only increase engagement, but to eradicate stereotypes and affirm their value as human beings (Russell, 2020).

In order to eradicate racism, we must provide our children with an education that includes all American history and that examines how that history continues to shape our institutions, beliefs and culture.

Bill Russell (2020)

How students are taught about slavery depends on the state they live in and the textbooks used. As recently as February 2019, reports of inconsistent and inaccurate historical facts about slavery in America were once again brought to light, this time by CBS News (Duncan, Luibrand & Zawistowski, 2020). Four textbooks used widely in public schools were examined and results included:

The omission of White supremacy as the ideology of the Confederate States.

Slaves being referred to as "immigrants"; inaccurate vocabulary used to describe enslaved labor to young school-aged children as "chores".

The intentional omission of key facts regarding American political figures who owned slaves; the belief of raping female slaves to increase slave holdings without cost to the slave owner.

Not identifying which American Presidents were segregationists. What textbook or primary sources does your school or district use to teach American history? Is the impact of slavery accurately portrayed?

The reinforcement of the inferiority of Black and Brown Americans is not just present in social studies curricula, but may also be found in other subject areas, including literacy resources. In the *Journal of Curriculum Studies*, a critical content analysis of Fountas and Pinnell's (F&P) leveled literacy intervention (LLI) uncovered a hidden curriculum that perpetuated oppressive ideologies (Thomas & Dyches, 2019). This widely used intervention resource presents racialized representations to students. In 70% of fiction and 20% of nonfiction F&P LLI books, people of color are presented as inferior, deviant, and/or helpless, while 30% of fiction and 100% of nonfiction F&P LLI books present Whites as heroic, determined, innovative, and successful.

As we think about eradicating the barrier of occupational hierarchy of our Black and Brown students, we have to identify the hidden curriculum within our resources that subconsciously reinforces the pathways to these barriers. When was the last time your school or district's curriculum and library resources were audited for diversity and accuracy of representation?

Action

The next step of eradicating occupational hierarchy for our Black and Brown students requires even more courage to initiate than assessing personal awareness and knowledge gaps of systemic racism in our country. We know that we need to target inequities in school practice, culture, and operations. By taking action, we can move schools and districts from rhetoric to the actual practice of addressing inequities.

Equity work is complex. No single person can affect this type of systemic change alone. How can schools and districts identify leaders, drivers, and access points to activate agency in all stakeholders? Just as many school districts engage in a fairly thorough process of developing its strategic plan, using a similar strategy to conduct an equity and diversity audit will highlight areas of opportunity to help eradicate occupational hierarchy.

Equity and Diversity Audit

Conducting an equity and diversity audit will help identify institutional policies and practices within a school or district that results in discriminatory data of minority students and a hostile work environment for diverse staff. This type of audit is especially critical due to COVID-19 school closures and remote learning.

Research suggests analyzing data in the following three key areas can help schools and districts find areas of concern that may require further investigation (Skrla et al, 2009):

1. Programmatic equity
2. Teaching quality equity
3. Achievement equity

The Intercultural Development Research Association (IDRA) provides guiding questions to support data collection around these three key areas to help schools and districts discover the institutional changes needed to ensure equitable, diverse and inclusive environments for all students (Johnson, 2020).

Programmatic equity	• Which population groups are underrepresented in Advanced Placement (AP) classes or honors classes? • Which groups are overrepresented or underrepresented in special education classes? • Which groups are disciplined more often and more severely than other groups?
Teaching quality equity	• Are the most experienced teachers teaching the students with the greatest needs? • Are most of the new teachers teaching in the schools with the greatest needs? • Are there certain schools where there is high teacher turnover? Why? • Are teachers in the high needs areas, like special education and bilingual education, certified?
Achievement equity	• Where are the achievement and opportunity gaps among population groups based on the state assessment exam at each grade level? • Which population groups are graduating at lower rates than others? • Which students are being retained? • Which students are dropping out of school?

An audit of this magnitude requires substantial feedback from all stakeholders. While the recent pandemic has altered how we teach and connect with students, families, and even fellow educators, be resourceful in your approach to ensure all stakeholders have the opportunity to provide meaningful input. Virtual listening sessions and focus groups from specific stakeholder groups can provide a diverse perspective of the level of equity and perception of diversity support.

Once the data has been collected and analyzed, the creation of precise action steps with clear indicators for how well schools and districts are meeting the diverse needs of their students is critical to ensure progress. Using goals that are (specific, measurable, attainable, results-oriented, and time-bound (SMART) as your action plan framework is one well established tool to plan and achieve your equity and diversity goals. To further address the occupational hierarchy, be sure to include explicit opportunities for students to shadow, and/or work in, or learn about career pathways based on their passions and areas of strength.

Reflection

Facing our biases does not lend itself to easy conversations. Race is a social construct embedded in the very creation of the US, with many of our forefathers juxtaposing revolutionary ideas of equality and human rights yet upholding slavery and ideas of race. As educators, we must be committed to initiate and facilitate productive, honest conversations about root causes of biases and the impact those biases have on our interactions with students, parents, and colleagues.

Reflection is a powerful tool in not only assessing the progress of our actions, but processing the reactions to our actions from our stakeholders. Here are a few questions to consider as you reflect on your next steps:

◆ How might you encourage the collective action of your colleagues to explore spaces for dialogue on diversity so all students feel safe and valued?

◆ When constructing space for dialogue, what norms should guide these conversations to ensure equal participation of all voices and freedom from judgement?

◆ Small groups of committed educators can drive change in school equity efforts. What action will you take next week to help lead the equity work in your school or district?

◆ How might you avoid structural inequities in your master schedule and student course request process to provide more equitable access and opportunities for diverse students groups.

♦ What can we do to support the healthy development of each of our students and ignite the courage of our communities for social change?

Divisive political discourse around race, religion, and immigration have frayed the seams of our communities in the US. It is imperative we have courageous conversations to repair the damage and take decisive action, opening pathways for our Black and Brown students to become more than "the help."

Resources

Angelou, M. (n.d.). Do the Best You Can Until You Know Better. Then When You Know Better, Do Better. *theysaidso.com*. Retrieved January 7, 2021, from https://theysaidso.com/quote/maya-angelou-do-the-best-you-can-until-you-know-better-then-when-you-know-better.

Balingit, M. and Meckler, L. (2020, September 18). Trump Alleges 'Left-Wing Indoctrination' in Schools, Says He Will Create National Commission to Push More 'Pro-American' History. *The Washington Post*. Retrieved December 1, 2020, from www.washingtonpost.com/education/trump-history-education/2020/09/17/f40535ec-ee2c-11ea-ab4e-581edb849379_story.html.

Brown, D. (2003). *The Da Vinci Code*. New York, NY: Doubleday.

Jericka Duncan, S., Luibrand, S. and Zawistowski, C. (2020, February 19). Map in Widely Used U.S. History Textbook Refers to Enslaved Africans as "Immigrants," CBS News Analysis Finds. *CBS News*. Retrieved December 1, 2020, from www.cbsnews.com/news/the-american-pageant-map-in-widely-used-us-history-textbook-refers-to-enslaved-africans-as-immigrants-cbs-news/.

Johnson, P.N. (2020, April). Using Equity Audits to Assess and Address Opportunity Gaps Across Education. *Intercultural Development Research Association*. Retrieved December 1, 2020, from www.idra.org/resource-center/using-equity-audits-to-assess-and-address-opportunity-gaps-across-education.

Piacenza, J. (2014, December 12). PRRI CEO Robert P. Jones Appears on the BBC. *Public Religion Research Institute*. Retrieved December 1, 2020, from www.prri.org/press-coverage/prri-ceo-robert-p-jones-appears-on-the-bbc/.

Project Implicit. (n.d.). Take a Test. Retrieved December 1, 2020, from https://implicit.harvard.edu/implicit/takeatest.html.

Russell, B. (2020, September 14). Racism Is Not a Historical Footnote. *The Players' Tribune*. Retrieved December 1, 2020, from www.theplayerstribune.com/articles/bill-russell-nba-racial-injustice.

Thomas, D. and Dyches, J. (2019). The Hidden Curriculum of Reading Intervention: A Critical Content Analysis of Fountas & Pinnell's Leveled Literacy Intervention. *Journal of Curriculum Studies*, *51*(5), 601–18. https://doi.org/10.1080/00220272.2019.1616116

Skrla, L., McKenzie, K.B., Scheurich, J.J. (Eds.). (2009). *Using Equity Audits to Create Equitable and Excellent Schools*. Thousand Oaks, CA: Corwin Press.

Afterword
It's All about Leadership

Jimmy Casas

> We cannot change what we are not aware of, and once we are aware, we cannot help but change.
>
> Sheryl Sandberg (2013)

There are three things that I have come to believe when it comes to leadership:

Leadership matters
It's all about leadership
Everyone is a leader

Leadership comes in many forms and looks different depending on the individual's experience, knowledge, skill sets, personal characteristics, and the severity and/or significance of the situation. Every time a decision is made, you lead. You lead when you initiate a conversation or contribute to a discussion. You lead when you present information or go out of your way to help a student with an assignment or lend a caring ear. You lead when you serve as an unofficial mentor to a colleague or when others notice your tendency to always see the best in others. You lead when you take great pride in or care deeply about your students, colleagues, and school. You lead when you recognize that everyone around you who's in a position to make decisions looks the same, yet the support, programs and resources provided for different people or groups look vastly different and you feel compelled to ask why. And, finally, you are a leader when once you recognize the inequities that exist within the organization, you feel a moral obligation to help change it. You cannot help but change, as the Sandberg quote says.

Throughout the book, our aim was to remind readers of the disparities that exist within our current practices, particularly, but not limited to voice, access, cultural capital, early childhood, after-school programming, grading and assessment, and intersectionality in the educational process. More importantly, our hope was to inspire you, the reader, to recognize and accept that change begins and ends with each of us.

Everything starts with leadership. In order to bring about significant change and ensure equity across all levels, we must look internally and be willing to examine the deepest parts of our traditions, our thinking, our conversations, our behaviors, and our current practices with the hope that we are willing to admit our own shortcomings, and, in some cases, openly celebrate our accomplishments. When we are in our most vulnerable state, our greatest opportunities are exposed—opportunities to assess, model, and promote equitable practices not only in dialogue, but also through our actions.

No longer is it acceptable for all staff not to see themselves as leaders. After all, everyone has the capacity to lead, regardless of their current position or title. We must be intentional in encouraging and inviting others to lead with us, both new and veteran staff alike. We must put structures in place to ensure that all staff continue to grow and develop so we can multiply our leadership capacity. Schools that place an emphasis on equitable opportunities are intentional in their recruitment, hiring, retainment, and advancement of staff with diverse backgrounds and compositions as it pertains to race, ethnicity, gender, sexual identity, and other characteristics. They establish structures to gauge the cultural challenges that many of our minority staff members face, including feelings of isolation and disconnection.

They examine attrition rates of both minority and White staff members. They put processes in place to ensure that they are not putting the same people in leadership positions, whether it be school improvement committees, grade level or department chair leaders, building leadership teams, instructional coaches, curriculum coordinators, or administrators. In other words, they are always mindful of dispersing opportunities in an equitable manner in order to cultivate a culture that reflects and promotes diversity. Students of all backgrounds need to see adults in the building who share their identities.

Here are a few things to consider in your efforts to empower and hopefully inspire a community of leaders to come together to lead:

1. Create a diversity or inclusion team to stimulate dialogue, identify areas of disconnect, create a sense of belonging, and inspire action that brings about positive resolutions.
2. Provide learning opportunities for veteran staff members to mentor, advise, model, and teach new team members, and for new staff to showcase their talents as soon as they are brought on board.
3. Disperse leadership opportunities so the same people are not being called on to lead time and time again. Invest in coaching conversations in order to build confidence and set all staff members up for success.
4. Create unified expectations for student learning together with all staff rather than telling staff what the learning outcomes will be.
5. Provide opportunities for all teachers and administrators to do classroom walk-throughs (partner observations) together in order to learn from one another.
6. Invite interdisciplinary teams of staff members to conduct site visits at other schools in order to learn from one another and share observations/findings with their colleagues.
7. Implement planning and co-presenting opportunities so teachers and administration can plan and teach together.

8. Allow for rotation of all staff to lead and facilitate grade level/department meetings, faculty meetings, building leadership meetings, and professional development trainings.

Many teachers, support staff, guest teachers, bus drivers, principals, and superintendents are leaving the education profession for a variety of reasons. Schools and districts across the country are experiencing shortages across the board at all levels, regardless of whether they are urban, rural, suburban, large, or small communities. We need to do everything in our power to retain our colleagues and recruit new colleagues, becoming intentional about hiring and retaining educators in all roles who represent the diverse student body we serve in our country. Barriers continue to exist for those who want to join the profession, but for educators and aspiring educators who are Black, Brown, gay, lesbian, transgender and nonbinary, they face even greater obstacles, including inadequate teacher preparation programs, isolation, cultural biases, lack of diversity on hiring committees, lack of ongoing support systems, college affordability, loan forgiveness programs, job placement programs, and lack of connectivity due to an overall lack of diversity. We must diligently invest time, resources, support, and guidance in our staff in order to understand their experiences so our connection remains strong and we can continue to lead and grow together.

The most effective educators didn't become teachers and principals to become successful. They became educators in order to influence the learning environment and conditions so students, staff, and aspiring educators alike could have an equal opportunity to create and experience their own successes. We all play a part in changing the narrative of what the role of the leader looks like. We cannot allow ourselves to get stuck in a closed mindset that defines the role of the principal as, "It is what it is and it's always been this way." If our intentions are to inspire others to follow our lead and pursue leadership positions, then we must do exactly that: Create more equitable opportunities for others to lead alongside us and tell our story in a way that truly reflects how wonderful this profession really is. The role a school leader plays in creating a culture of equity doesn't have to look like it has always looked like or be what others want it to be or what they believe it should be.

Undoubtedly, there are a plethora of issues facing us in education today that can burden us and paralyze us to remain stagnant or worse yet, blame others for our lack of success. I recognize that being an effective leader is not simply about being able to inspire others through our words or actions. Nothing is that simple, especially when it comes to leadership. Successful leaders recognize that everyone in an organization has strengths, skills, and talents that, if cultivated, can help move a school forward in a more efficient, effective, and equitable manner. The ability to draw on the diversity of the collective knowledge and wisdom of all staff members and then lean on them to help navigate potentially treacherous issues are traits effective leaders possess. By investing in others, you will learn it's not about a title, but about making a significant difference in each other. Reset your mindset so that you see your role as an equity director, a builder of people who utilizes the talents, skills, knowledge, and disposition of all staff, regardless of background, to influence them in ways so they not only see themselves as leaders, but others recognize them as leaders and want to emulate them. At its core, equity simply means giving each person what they need to succeed. Often, when considering the virtuous idea of giving each person what they need to succeed in schools, our first thoughts go to students, and ensuring that we provide each student we serve with what they need to succeed as individual humans and individual learners. This is, of course, noble and as it should be. Yet, we must not forget about the adults in the schools who serve these students. Each adult in a school is as unique as each student and we must do everything in our power to provide them with equitable opportunities. In order to provide equitable learning experiences for our students, as leaders, we must model this by providing equitable opportunities to succeed for those we lead. We will never achieve equity in our schools without strong and equitable leadership practices, including ensuring that all educators have the opportunity to lead.

As I mentioned previously, there are three things that I have come to believe when it comes to leadership:

Leadership matters
It's all about leadership
Everyone is a leader

In considering these three beliefs through an equity lens, I believe these three things even more strongly. In our schools, equity matters as much as leadership matters. In fact, it may be even more important. However, it will never happen in the absence of leadership. Effecting change of any kind in our schools—or our society at large—requires strong leaders and strong leadership. Achieving equity in our schools is all about leadership. And it simply cannot happen if only some of us lead. The issue of equity is too important—and, in fact, too daunting—to think it will happen unless each of us plays an active leadership role in promoting and, eventually, achieving it.

Resource

Sandberg, S. (2013). *Lean in: Women, Work, and the Will to Lead.* New York: Alfred A. Knopf.

For Product Safety Concerns and Information please contact our
EU representative GPSR@taylorandfrancis.com Taylor & Francis
Verlag GmbH, Kaufingerstraße 24, 80331 München, Germany